A HISTORY OF LEICESTERSHIRE AND RUTLAND

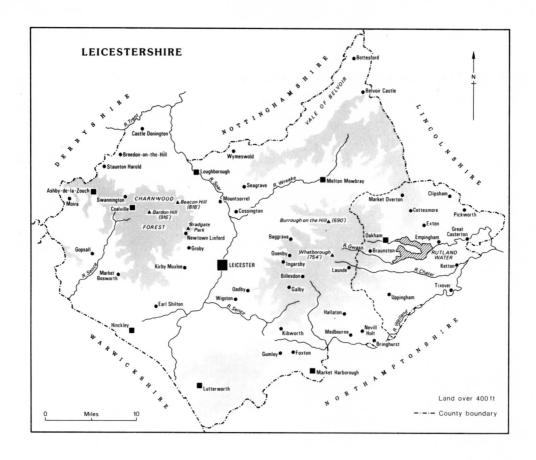

LEICESTERSHIRE

DERBYSHIRE

NOTTINGHAMSHIRE

VALE OF BELVOIR

LINCOLNSHIRE

WARWICKSHIRE

NORTHAMPTONSHIRE

N

• Bottesford

• Belvoir Castle

• Castle Donington

• Breedon-on-the-Hill

• Staunton Harold

■ Loughborough

• Wymeswold

• Seagrave

R. Wreake

■ Melton Mowbray

R. Soar

• Ashby-de-la-Zouch

• Swannington

CHARNWOOD

• Moira

• Coalville

▲ Beacon Hill (818')

▲ Bardon Hill (916')

FOREST

'Bradgate Park ▲

Newtown Linford

• Groby

• Mountsorrel

• Cossington

Burrough on the Hill ▲ (690')

• Market Overton

• Clipsham

• Cottesmore

• Pickworth

• Exton

• Oakham

Great Casterton

• Empingham

RUTLAND WATER

R. Gwash

• Braunston

R. Chater

• Ketton

• Gopsall

R. Sence

• Market Bosworth

Kirby Muxloe •

■ LEICESTER

• Baggrave

• Quenby

• Ingarsby

Whatborough (754') ▲

• Billesdon

• Galby

• Launde

• Tixover

• Earl Shilton

• Oadby

• Wigston

R. Sence

■ Hinckley

• Kibworth

• Gumley

• Foxton

• Galby

• Medbourne

Hallaton •

Nevill Holt •

• Bringhurst

• Uppingham

R. Welland

■ Market Harborough

■ Lutterworth

0   Miles   10

Land over 400 ft

—·—·— County boundary

R. Trent

THE DARWEN COUNTY HISTORY SERIES

A History of Leicestershire and Rutland

ROY MILLWARD

Drawings by Helen Millward

Cartography by Ruth Rowell and Kate Moore

PHILLIMORE

1985

Published by
PHILLIMORE & CO. LTD.
Shopwyke Hall, Chichester, Sussex

ISBN 0 85033 390 3

Printed in Great Britain at the
University Press, Oxford

Contents

Decorated urn, Church Langton

Acknowledgements

Cruck-framed house, Newton Linford

A book such as this can be written only with the help of many others. I am particularly grateful for the help of friends and colleagues in Leicester University. Kenneth Garfield and his staff in the Photographic Unit there have been unstinting in their technical advice, and from the author's negatives they have conjured up a magnificent series of prints, some involving the difficult transformation of colour transparencies into black-and-white pictures. Terry Garfield, in charge of technical facilities in the Geography Department at Leicester University, has been of assistance in countless ways and two members of his staff, Ruth Rowell and Kate Moore, have drawn the excellent set of maps that illuminate the text.

Over the years I have visited every parish in Leicestershire and Rutland and for this I am ever grateful to my wife who, following the traditions of local historians, has driven the car to all these places. An even greater debt of gratitude is owing to my wife, Helen, for the hundred-and-odd line-drawings that she has made to decorate and convey further information in the margins of the book. Finally, one cannot write a book of this kind, a succession of snapshots over a vast span of time, without recourse to the works of many who have delved into the past of the two counties. In the brief bibliography at the end of the book I mention the publications that have been of particular importance in the making of this synthesis of Leicestershire and Rutland.

List of Plates

List of Maps

ACKNOWLEDGEMENTS: MAPS

1. P. Liddle, *Leicestershire Archaeology*, Vol. I, 1982; 2. Liddle, *Leicestershire Archaeology*, Vol. II, 1982; 3. K. M. Kenyon, *TLAS*, 26, 1948 and J. S. Wacher, *TLAHS*, 52, 1976; 4. as 2; 5. D. Holly, *TLAS*, 20, 1939 and I. B. Terrett, *The Domesday Geography of Midland England*, 1954; 6. C. T. Smith, *Population of Leicestershire*, 1955 and I. B. Terrett, as above; 7. B. H. Cox, *TLAHS*, 47, 1971; 8. C. D. B. Ellis, *History in Leicester*, 1969; 9. L. M. Cantor, *TLAHS*, 46, 1970; 10. W. G. Hoskins, *Leicestershire*, 1957; 11. W. G. Hoskins, *TLAHS*, 1956; 15. C. T. Smith, *The City of Leicester*, 1958; 16. Survey of Leicester, 1983; Leicester City Council and Leicestershire County Council.
(For abbreviations *see* bibliography.)

Preface

This sketch of the histories of two English counties looks back over more than 2,000 years, a backward glance that is made possible only because of the great number of enquiring minds that have paid attention to this part of the Midlands. The long road of research in Leicestershire's local history has several outstanding landmarks. John Nichols at the close of the 18th century provided a ground plan for all later work in the six volumes of his topographical history. The end of the 19th century saw the beginning of an even more thorough investigation of Leicestershire's past in *The Victoria County History* whose publication is not yet complete after more than 50 years. Of equal importance in the promotion of local research was the foundation of the Leicestershire Archaeological Society. The years since the Second World War have witnessed another notable advance in Leicestershire research. The founding of the Department of English Local History at the University College, the only one of its kind in any British university, created a focus of local studies. Alongside the research in several departments of the university, investigations directed by the Leicester museums have transformed our knowledge of the county's archaeology and prehistory. But the most radical of recent changes derives not from any academic discoveries, but from the immense powers of central government that resulted, in 1974, in the extinction of Rutland – an independent area of administration that had been in existence since the 12th century. Officially Rutland is now part of Leicestershire, but the axe that fell in 1974 has served only to strengthen local feeling for this small county and its unique personality. Signs by the road side still announce that one is about to drive into Rutland and a local society, the Rutland Record Society, was founded in 1979. One piece of this new society's work is the publication of a handsome journal, 'Rutland Record'. If those nameless planners of the new counties in the early 1970s had given more thought to the past they might have come up with a different answer to the problems of local government and economic organisation in the latter half of the 20th century. Rutland might have expanded eastward to swallow up part of Lincolnshire and the historic town of Stamford, a place as worthy as any of the role of a regional capital in the East Midlands.

St John Baptist, King's Norton

Old slate quarry, Swithland

I The Landscape

The counties of Rutland and Leicestershire together encompass some of the most attractive landscapes of the East Midlands. The western boundary of Leicestershire has marched along the line of Roman Watling Street ever since the county took shape before the Norman Conquest. To the east an even more ancient feature of the countryside, the prehistoric Sewstern Lane, divides Leicestershire from Lincolnshire. Another Roman road, Ermine Street, runs close to the eastern border of Rutland. The country that lies between these ancient routes to the north has long formed the heart of the East Midlands. Here lay the tribal territories of the Coritani, the native British whom the Romans found in possession of the land. Eight centuries later in time the same region lay at the heart of the Danelaw when the Scandinavian armies settled the land and established two of their military capitals at Stamford and Leicester. The southern and northern limits of Leicestershire and Rutland stretch out towards two of the eastward flowing rivers of the Midlands. The Welland acts as a boundary with Northamptonshire in the south, while Leicestershire looks northward to the wide plain of the Trent. But only about the outfall of its own chief river, the Soar, does the county reach the banks of this greatest waterway of the north Midlands. Rivers, apart from the Soar, play a part of no importance in the topography of these two East Midland counties. Here we are concerned with a landscape of uplands in miniature where streams of little-known names – Chater, Gwash, Wreake and Sence – make their lazy ways towards the Trent and Welland, the Tame and Warwickshire Avon.

The heights of Leicestershire and Rutland reach higher than most travellers through the Midlands might imagine. Bardon Hill with its 912 feet above sea level on the western flank of the Charnwood Forest is unimpressive as the highest point of Leicestershire, its slopes gashed by one of the county's biggest quarries and within sight and sound of the continuous roar of the M1's traffic. The panorama of the Midland landscape that opens up from the summit of Bardon Hill at least established the centrality of Leicestershire. The writers of Victorian guide-books with their love of topographical detail could enthuse over this prospect. As one of them wrote, 'the declivities of this hill are well wooded, and the summer house on its summit commands perhaps a more extensive prospect than any eminence of the same altitude in the kingdom. Belvoir Castle, Lincoln Cathedral (at a distance of 45 miles), the Peak Hills of Derbyshire, and Coventry spires may all be seen on a

The Hanging Stone,
The Oaks,
Charnwood
Forest

11

clear day, and sometimes the Malvern Hills of Worcestershire; the whole range of vision embracing an area of 5000 square miles'.

In west Leicestershire view-points and quarrying seem to be inevitably joined. At Breedon-on-the-Hill, at the northern extremity of the county overlooking the broad valley of the Trent, the harsh precipitous face of a huge quarry in the carboniferous limestone has moved forward relentlessly destroying, since the beginning of this century, more than a third of the area of this shapely hill. Doubtless Breedon's history will save this landmark and look-out in the Leicestershire landscape, for its summit is the site of a Saxon monastery that was mentioned by Bede early in the eighth century and there, on this land that was hallowed before the Danish raiders followed the line of the Trent into the heart of the Midlands, stands one of our most important medieval churches.

East Leicestershire and Rutland may not quite reach the heights of the summits that lie to the west of the Soar, but there is a greater sense of space in the embracing prospects. The highest places, on the lip of the Marlstone escarpment, lie at more than 700 feet above the sea and all present wide views of the surrounding Leicestershire wolds, a varied landscape of little hills, intricate valleys, splashed with the dark patches of fox coverts and everywhere the faint patterns of ridge and furrow — the last visible signs of the medieval open fields. Eastward again, the proportions of the physical landscape are reduced in scale, a change that would seem to match the dimensions of England's smallest county. Even so, there is a spaciousness, almost a grandeur, about the prospect from the crest of the Lincolnshire limestone escarpment where it looks across the Vale of Catmose, between Market Overton and Burley, although the highest parts barely surpass 400 feet above sea level. The same sense of space under big skies is felt in the south-eastern corner of the county where the long ridges by Ketton and Empingham fall away gently towards the unrelieved flatness of Fenland.

The landscapes of Leicestershire and Rutland form a bridge between the West Midlands and eastern England; similarly they are composed of geological elements of both these regions. The valley of the Soar creates the great divide in the geological make-up of this East Midland core. To the west of the Soar corridor, below Leicester, the oldest rocks of the county, indeed some of the oldest rocks of the British Isles, protrude through the rich red marls and sandstones of Triassic age that form the characteristically warm, coloured countrysides of the West Midlands. Eastward of the dividing Soar younger clays and limestones, gently dipping towards the North Sea basin, underlie the broad clay vales or stand out as sinuous escarpments. Take Leicestershire and Rutland together and the traveller will find samples of the geology of many parts of England. West Leicestershire alone contains a tiny outcrop of the carboniferous limestone that appears so extensively in the Pennines to the north, a coalfield whose outer seams, revealed at the surface around Coleorton, were already being worked in the Middle Ages, and the relics, in Charnwood Forest, of the outpourings of a volcano that take the mind back to the remotest epochs of geological time.

12

The ancient rocks of Charnwood Forest are exposed over an area of some seven miles by five to the north-west of the city of Leicester. Seven hundred million years ago, in pre-Cambrian times, volcanic activity at a centre that seems to have been located towards the north-western fringe of the Forest poured lavas and deposited ash into unknown seas. The sediments of these times, 10,000 feet and more in thickness it is believed, were changed under pressure in the earth movements that folded the whole succession of rocks into a broad arch-like structure that plunges in a south-easterly direction. Beside the volcanic ash, much of it redeposited under water as mudstones, the breccias or 'bomb rocks' of the violent periods of vulcanicity and the lava flows, the complex geology of Charnwood Forest at the present time also reveals materials from the earth's interior that solidified at greater depths. These are the diorites that were intruded at a later date in the evolution of the basement rocks of this part of the Midlands. Today the location of these hard rocks can be recognised in the distribution of the quarrying for road stone on the western fringe of the Forest. The last phase in the emplacement of the rocks that make up Charnwood Forest was the intrusion in Silurian times, some 400 million years ago, of the grey and pink granite of Mountsorrel. Today the exposure of the geological foundations of Leicestershire in Charnwood Forest occupies only a tiny fraction of the area of the county. Even within the 11,000 acres of Charnwood, the outcrop of the old rocks is far from continuous; they form a succession of island-like projections through the cover of Keuper Marl.

Watts in his classic account of the geology of Charnwood Forest described the region as a mountain range that had been sculptured and then buried beneath the accumulating sands of deserts in Triassic times, some 200 million years ago. The landscape that we now see of dark weathered crags at Beacon Hill, High Sharpley and beside the road that follows the western heights of the Forest from Markfield to Whitwick, Watts saw as an exhumed landscape from those distant times – the fossilised landforms of the Triassic age. Later workers have come to consider the lines of rugged tors that occur along the outcrops of ancient hard rocks in the Forest as products of the much more recent severe sub-Arctic climates of the Ice Age. In this view, the tors are rocky outcrops severely frost-shattered in the cold climates of 20,000 years ago. Doubtless much still awaits elucidation, but of the role of this landscape in the history of Leicestershire there is little doubt. The Romans quarried the Swithland slates and we find the same material down the centuries into the Victorian age in the gravestones of Leicestershire churchyards many miles removed from the quarries of the Brand and Woodhouse Eaves. And today these complex little hills with their intrusions of diorite and granite are the reason for one of Leicestershire's important industries, the production of road-stone for a market in a large area of the south-east Midlands.

Charnwood
Tor

Apart from the intricacies of the solid geology of Charnwood, the most complex structures and variety of rock types lie in the north and

13

west of the county. Here the main geological divisions of the southern Pennines, the carboniferous limestone, the millstone grit and the coal measures, occur in a very different topographical setting from that of the high central plateau and bold escarpments of the Peak District. The limestone is found in a series of tiny 'inliers' or exposures through the younger covering rocks, the red marls of Triassic age. Breedon Hill is the most obvious representative of the carboniferous limestone. The coal-bearing rocks contain about 20 worthwhile seams that outcrop in two small separate coalfields. The Leicestershire coalfield lies to the east of Ashby de la Zouch. Around Coleorton and Swannington the coal measures are exposed at the surface. Camden, the great topographer and antiquarian of Elizabeth I's time, in his account of Coleorton, the residence of Henry de Beaumont, records that coal mining there 'yields much profit to the Lord of the Manor, and supplies all the neighbourhood far and near with fireing'. Nowadays active mining is limited to the buried part of the coalfield from Coalville southwards where the seams plunge ever deeper beneath the red Triassic rocks. To the west of Ashby de la Zouch, on the very western fringe of the county, the coal seams and their accompanying brick and tile clays of the South Derbyshire coalfield project into Leicestershire. Measham, Donisthorpe and Moira are the chief mining villages. Here the crooked walls, the crazy angles of doors and windows, as well as the strapped and splintered buildings, speak of a degree of subsidence that would match the heavily-mined areas of the Black Country.

The river Soar and its tributaries occupy a wide plain that covers the greater part of central Leicestershire. The underlying rocks are composed of a thick series of red mudstones, the Keuper marls, that reach a thickness of almost a thousand feet and the lowest division of the Jurassic, made up of the clays and thin bands of limestone belonging to the lower lias. But these rocks belong to the solid geology of central Leicestershire; almost everywhere they are hidden by the clays, gravels and sands that were deposited by the ice sheets of the Quaternary Age. In many places the boulder clays of the glaciation reach scores of feet in thickness. Borings, for instance, in South Leicestershire have shown that the drift lies to a thickness of well over 200 feet.

In the most eastern parts of Leicestershire and in Rutland the more varied elements of the solid geology influence the topography of the present landscape. Across the borderland between the two counties from Belvoir Castle to the miniature wooded heights of the Laughton Hills near Market Harborough, the marlstone rock bed, a hard band of iron bearing limestone belonging to the division of the middle lias, gives rise to a rolling plateau landscape and, in places, sharply etched westward-facing escarpments. Geologically this is a complex landscape because of the skin of glacial deposits that so often masks the underlying solid geology. But the marlstone rock gives a unity to the landscape that man has shaped out of the hill country of the Leicestershire-Rutland border over the past thousand years. Its use as a building stone, in churches, barns, cottages and mansions has given a rich, honey-coloured glow to this cool green countryside.

In Rutland and on the easternmost border of Leicestershire the underlying rocks repeat the patterns of the marlstone country. Here the clays of the upper lias underlie harder formations of the Northampton sand ironstone and the Lincolnshire limestone. The scenery of Rutland can be understood in the pattern that these rocks make on the ground. The plain around Oakham, the Vale of Catmose, belongs to the outcrop of the clays. The sharply defined escarpment to the east, crowned by the noble mansion at Burley, marks the outcrop of the Northampton sand ironstone. The same rock forms the peninsula of Upper Hambleton that rises between the arms of Rutland Water and the long ridges that fall gently eastward to the Fenland from the hill country around Uppingham largely belong to the same iron bearing Northampton Sands. The easternmost parts of Rutland and the bleak upland of north-east Leicestershire beyond Waltham on the Wolds are composed of the Lincolnshire limestone. On this featureless plateau where surface streams are few, the long low horizons and the overwhelming sky create a sense of space. This is a countryside of famous building stones from Clipsham and Ketton, a countryside whose rich soils were sought out by the founders of villa estates in Roman Britain. In the villages of eastern Rutland the penetrating brilliance of spring sunshine seems to be magnified by the limestone walls of cottage and churches. Here one might find in Clipsham, Pickworth and Market Overton an England that had never known the industrial revolution but for the shattering noise of military jet aircraft, a reminder of Rutland's role in 20th-century Britain.

The Belvoir escarpment seen from the Vale

15

II Prehistory – The First Evidence of Man

*Sewstern Lane –
a prehistoric
trackway that forms,
in part, the boundary
between Leicestershire
and Lincolnshire*

Leicestershire and Rutland possess none of the famous eye-catching monuments of prehistory. Chambered tombs, stone circles, 'henge' monuments, barrow clusters, all are notably lacking, at least as surviving visible objects in the countryside. Not until the Iron Age, when the East Midlands formed the tribal territory of the people known to the Romans as the Coritani, did prehistoric man leave a permanent and impressive mark on the landscape. Only with the raising of the hill forts at Breedon and Burrough is it possible to record man's contribution to the shaping of the Leicestershire environment.

The absence of any striking man-made landscape features from the time before the Iron Age coupled with the paucity of many of the artifacts of early man – stone hammers, scrapers, arrow-heads, pottery and tools and weapons of bronze and copper – led earlier students of the archaeology of the East Midlands to dismiss the greater part of Leicestershire and Rutland as a region empty and neglected by the prehistoric peoples of Britain. For instance, when *The Victoria History of the Counties of England* began publication at the beginning of this century, there was no firm evidence of the presence of Palaeolithic man in this part of the Midlands. The author of the section on *Early Man* in Rutland was able to write 'of remains of the Palaeolithic period it is perhaps questionable whether Rutland is likely to yield any examples'. But research in recent years has been able to correct this view. A number of flint implements, mainly from the gravel terraces of the Soar and Wreake, testifies to the presence of Palaeolithic and Mesolithic hunting communities. A hand-axe from Ratcliffe-on-the-Wreake and flint flakes from Wanlip have been dated to an interglacial period of the Ice Age between 70,000 and 100,000 years ago. Another long blank in the prehistoric calendar that has been filled by research over recent years, appears in evidence for the presence of Mesolithic man, in hunting groups that wandered through the forests in the time between the end of the Ice Age and the impact of the first farmers on the Atlantic coastlands after 4000 B.C. Microliths, the distinctive tiny flint blades of the Mesolithic hunters, have been found during the 1950s and 1960s at Leicester, Stoney Stanton and Burrough. For the first time there is a hint of a place that was occupied and used by early man. At Ratcliffe-on-the-Wreake a group of flint implements of Mesolithic age was discovered in 1951, and it is believed that here was a spot where the raw material was shaped and worked up into useful tools.

16

1. Bradgate Park — this medieval deer park first appears in the documentary record in 1247 when it is mentioned in an agreement over hunting rights in Charnwood Forest between Roger de Quincy, Earl of Winchester, and Roger de Sumery, Baron of Dudley. Here are the oldest trees in Leicestershire, oaks that may date back to the time of the building of Bradgate House about 1500.

2. Bradgate Park — a medieval deer park that became the Leicestershire estate of the Grey family. Marquesses of Dorset and later Earls of Stamford. After the abandonment of Bradgate House as a residence the park still remained a hunting ground through the 19th century. Today the Park is one of the county's chief places of recreation. There are nature trails, a museum in the former chapel of Bradgate House, and deer still wander there.

3. and 4. Breedon-on-the-Hill, the church of St Mary and St Hardulph contains 30 fragments of Saxon sculpture whose date is believed to belong to the late eighth century. The sculpture from the Saxon monastery, named by Bede as *Brindun*, is set in strips in the walls of the medieval church; (*above*) The Virgin; (*below*) 'big-bellied beast'.

5. Breedon-on-the-Hill — the squat tower of St Mary and St Hardulph peeps above the face of the limestone quarry — a face whose advance over the past 30 years has removed much of the rampart of the Iron Age camp.

6. The hill of Breedon looks out over the Vale of Trent. Here the north face remains, up to now, immune from the advancing limestone quarry. The Bulwarks, the rampart of an Iron Age settlement, is marked by the hedgerow in front of the church, itself occupying the ground of the eighth-century Mercian monastery of *Brindun*.

7. The ruins of Bradgate House, built between 1490 and 1500, by Thomas Grey, Marquis of Dorset. It was one of England's unfortified great houses that, by the time of the Tudors, began to take the place of the castles of the aristocracy. Bradgate gradually decayed through the 18th century after the Greys, Earls of Stamford, took up their chief residence at Enville, Staffordshire.

8. The Hall, standing within an irregular earthwork, is all that remains of Oakham Castle. It was built by Walkelin de Ferrers, probably between 1180 and 1190, though no document survives to prove its date. Behind the screen of trees the 14th century tower of All Saints dominates the little capital of Rutland.

As one ponders over a map showing the distribution of the location in Leicestershire of the find spots of these objects from the Palaeolithic and Mesolithic periods, one is impressed by a pattern that picks out the north-south corridor of the river Soar. Were groups of Old Stone Age hunters encamped on the banks of this Leicestershire river or have the floods of the proto-Soar carried these implements from unknown locations in its headwater territory? On the other hand, that same map perhaps depicts little more than the present state of our knowledge, a picture that shows the concentration of archaeological interest and research in and about the city of Leicester.

The obscurity that surrounds the earliest epochs of prehistory is scarcely relieved when we come to consider the Neolithic period – the age of the first farming communities – in Leicestershire and Rutland. Until the closing centuries of the Neolithic, after 2000 B.C., no pottery has yet come to light. The grander objects of the Neolithic world, long barrows and communal burial places in chambered tombs, are completely lacking. Only the most durable objects of Neolithic society, stone axes and hammers as well as flint arrowheads, blades and scrapers, have survived to testify to almost 2,000 years of prehistory in these parts of the East Midlands. More than 50 polished stone axes and hammers from the Neolithic period have now been recovered. In the past quarter century the greatest step forward in the study of these objects has been the recognition, through petrographical analysis, of the quarries, often in distant parts of Britain, from which the axes originated. For instance, four of the Neolithic axes found in Leicester have come from the prehistoric quarry that was discovered, some 30 years ago, close to the summit of the Langdale Pikes, in the Lake District. Another Neolithic axe factory, at Graig Lwyd overlooking the Menai Strait in North Wales, has been the origin of implements found in Leicester and at Glenfield. From even further afield is an axe that was picked up from the surface of the soil at Sharnford in 1971. Shaped out of a greenstone, its source of origin proved to be a gabbro that outcrops below the high tide level in Mount's Bay, near Penzance, in Cornwall. In other parts this type of Cornish axe has been associated with a kind of pottery that was being made about the end of the third millennium B.C. The presence in Leicestershire of Neolithic axes shaped out of rocks from remote parts of Britain suggests that some kind of trade existed between the farming communities of these islands more than 4,000 years ago.

The ability to recognise with accuracy the origins of the rocks from which these ancient implements were hewn has revealed the presence of axe factories close to the borders of Leicestershire. An important centre lay on the narrow outcrop of hard pre-Cambrian rocks to the south of Nuneaton. Axe hammers from this source have turned up in Leicester, Barrow-on-Soar and Ratcliffe-on-the-Wreake. Even more intriguing is the recognition of more local sources, in Charnwood Forest, in the manufacture of axes. Two axes, found at Spring Barrow Lodge, near Whitwick, are made of rock from the Blackbrook Series in the northern parts of the Forest. Another implement, found at Goadby Marwood in east Leicestershire, is derived from the Beacon series of the pre-Cambrian rocks of Charnwood Forest. Even more striking perhaps is the evidence of the axe that was found on the lower slopes of High Sharpley, only half a mile from the source of its parent rock in Strawberry Plantations, close beside the Blackbrook reservoir. Here is proof that Neolithic man was exploiting the subtle differences in the geology of Leicestershire to serve his economic needs. For the rest one can only speculate about the life and economy of the earliest farmers in the East Midlands, projecting on to this region ideas that have been worked out from the richer evidence of these times surviving in other parts of the British Isles. In their distribution, however, the Neolithic axes show a marked concentration around Leicester. Once again it is unclear whether this implies that this part of the Soar valley was already a cleared and settled tract from which centuries of continuous and intensive occupation have obliterated all evidence of Neolithic times apart from a handful of indestructible stone implements, or whether the clearance of building sites and the interest of professional and amateur archaeologists have brought to light objects that elsewhere lie concealed under the pastures of the East Midland countryside.

Pottery appears in the archaeological record of Leicestershire and Rutland only in the closing centuries of the Neolithic between 1900 and 1650 B.C. Long-necked beakers associated with burials seem to mark the intrusion of an alien culture, that of the Beaker people, from across the North Sea. Seven beakers have been found in Leicestershire and their distribution suggests a colonising group that used the Welland valley and, to the north, the Lincolnshire Witham as paths of entry. Already the links of Leicestershire and Rutland with the river valleys leading to the Wash that was to remain a strong influence in the history of the region are evident at the threshold of the Bronze Age in the proposed cultural connections of the Beaker sites. But one must remember that these are sparse and inadequate facts on which to base a mass movement of prehistoric folk.

The Bronze Age lasted for 1,000 years and in this part of the Midlands the evidence of man's presence is as incomplete and unexciting as that from the earlier periods of prehistory. There are no stone circles or clustered groups of burial mounds, let alone the visible marks of field-systems and the evidence of settlement that we find in other parts of Britain. Bronze daggers, spearheads, cremation urns and fragments of pottery testify to the presence of man here between 1600 and 500 B.C. Three important collections of metal objects, dating from the later part of the Bronze Age, have long provided clues to this period. The Market Bosworth hoard, which is now lost, consisted of items – socketed axes, chisels and gouges – that might have formed the tool-kit of a carpenter. The axes, sword, bowl and parts of a bronze cauldron that make up the Welby hoard rank as the most important evidence of the Bronze Age that has until now been found in Leicestershire. Its bronzes include

Late Neolithic drinking vessel

18

designs of metal work that cannot be matched elsewhere in Britain. The cultural links of the finds at Welby are with Central Europe; its implications are of trade far beyond the confines of the East Midlands. The third collection of bronzes comes from Beacon Hill, one of Leicestershire's most visited viewpoints on the eastern fringe of Charnwood Forest. Beacon Hill's summit is ringed around with the faint trace of a rampart that has always been dated to the Iron Age. The discovery of a Bronze Age hoard within this earthwork suggests that the occupation of the hilltop and, perhaps, the hill fort itself, may date back before the Iron Age.

Since the Second World War a new aid to archaeological research, aerial photography, has been increasingly employed. Under the right condition of light and especially in periods of drought shadowy hidden features of the landscapes of prehistory are revealed from the air as crop marks and slight colorations of the soil. In Leicestershire new and unexpected objects of the Bronze Age landscape have already come to light. In the 1950s, a barrow showed up as a ring mark in the soil at Lockington, close to the river Trent. Excavation confirmed its Bronze Age date and an analysis of the buried surface beneath the barrow showed that the land had been burned and ploughed before the erection of the burial cairn. Aerial reconnaissance in recent years has revealed the faint marks of many ancient and long-obliterated landscape features. For instance, around Uppingham, between the valley of the Chater and the Eye Brook, a pattern of field-systems that predates the medieval ridge and furrow has been recognised. Most important, and dating back to the centuries of the late Neolithic and the early Bronze Age, the shapes of long vanished 'henge' monuments have been discerned. Among these, one is to be found at High Cross, on the western border of Leicestershire, close to the junction of the two main Roman roads across the Midlands, Watling Street and the Fosse Way.

Bronze Age cremation urns from Mountsorrel

19

III The Coritani and the Romans

In the fifth century B.C. the people of eastern and southern Britain
began to use iron in the manufacture of tools and weapons. Distinctive
and recognisable styles of pottery were part of this first Iron Age culture,
labelled by prehistorians for the purpose of classification as Iron Age
A. The beginnings of this most important period in the prehistory of the
British Isles are blurred and indefinite in this region of the Midlands.
Up to the present no satisfactory proof of the intrusion of an Iron Age
A culture into the territories of the two counties has been forthcoming.
Until recently the earliest suggestions of the period took the form of
pottery from several sites, including the great hill fort at Breedon, that
was dated to the decades about 200 B.C. and equated with the period of
Iron Age B. The most striking evidence from the three centuries before
the Roman conquest in the landscape belongs to the rare ditched and
embanked enclosures on two of Leicestershire's prominent hill-tops
at Burrough-on-the-Hill and Breedon. Two bouts of archaeological
investigation at the latter site, in 1946 and 1957, have shown the
continuous occupation of this hill-top from the second century B.C.
through the Roman period and on into the post-Roman centuries. Until
the present day scarcely any archaeological investigation has been made
of the even more impressive earthworks of Burrough-on-the-Hill, a
place that has been proposed, somewhat romantically, as the political
forerunner of Leicester in the tribal geography of the Iron Age.

Romano-British urn,
late fourth century,
Great Casterton

Leicestershire has only two undoubted Iron Age forts and there are
no such features in the landscape of Rutland. Here the prehistoric
geography of the East Midlands contrasts sharply with some parts of
the West Midlands and the Welsh border country, where the earthworks
of Iron Age enclosures seem to belong to almost every parish. Admittedly
the list of hill forts in Leicestershire and Rutland may be increased to
about half-a-dozen when the names of some as yet unproved sites are
added. Beacon Hill is the most certain of the sites in question. Life
Hill, near Billesdon, has been tentatively listed among the Iron Age
enclosures and Robin-a-Tiptoe has been proposed as the place where
the making of a hill fort was started at some time before the Roman
Conquest but never brought to completion. In Rutland it seems not
unlikely that an earthwork of the Iron Age once existed at Market
Overton. There the parish church has been raised within a rectangular-
shaped earth rampart close to the crest of the limestone escarpment that
overlooks the Vale of Catmose. This ancient landscape feature, largely

20

on the grounds of its formal rectangular shape, has been described as a Roman camp, but in the present state of our knowledge about the prehistory of Market Overton it could just as well be ascribed to the Iron Age tribe, the Coritani, who occupied the greater part of the East Midlands at the time of the Roman Conquest.

Iron Age forts, scarce as they are, form the last surviving visible features in the landscape of the people, the Coritani, whose society had been evolving here since the beginning of the second century B.C. Aerial photography has revealed much more evidence of early man in Leicestershire and Rutland. But the outlines of settlements on air photographs provide no precise evidence for their age. Along the Welland valley and from the terraces of the Trent and Soar the abundance of prehistoric markings, dating from any time between the Neolithic and the Romano-British centuries, must contain a substantial testimony of the Coritani and their occupation of the land that continued without break through the four centuries of Roman rule in these islands.

The Roman incursion into the territory of the Coritani took place in the years between A.D.43 and A.D.47. A generation followed in which the Roman legions organised the military occupation of the Midlands, but soon after A.D.70 the frontier of conquest stretched far to the north and west into the tribal lands of the Brigantes in the northern Pennines and in the mountain fastness of Wales. Leicestershire and Rutland ceased to have any military importance. The East Midlands entered upon more than three centuries of history in which Roman and British elements were closely intertwined. The countryside reveals scattered evidence of Coritanian villages and isolated farms, droveways and Roman roads, villas, places where iron ores were worked and smelted, small towns such as Great Casterton and a thriving regional capital, *Ratae Coritanorum*, that centuries later was to be known as Leicester.

The Roman roads of Leicestershire and Rutland were probably defined in the first years of the conquest primarily for military purposes. For instance, the Fosse Way seems to form an axis in the human geography of Leicestershire as important as the natural division of the line of the river Soar in the physical geography of the county. Among historians of Roman Britain the Fosse Way has long been considered as a temporary frontier in the occupation of these islands. Views on the exact nature of that frontier and the making of the Fosse Way have changed as fresh facts were brought to light. R.G. Collingwood, in the 1920s, was struck by the many miles of straight alignment in the course of the road between Exeter and Lincoln and concluded that the road had been surveyed and laid out in its entirety in the earliest years of the Roman occupation of Britain, before the tide of conquest extended into the north Midlands. Subsequent research on Roman Britain has modified views on the evolution of this temporary Midland frontier. T. Davies Pryce has argued that the road was constructed in two sections – the earliest part from Exeter to Leicester with a later projection from Leicester to Lincoln completed in the time of Scapula. Of late Graham

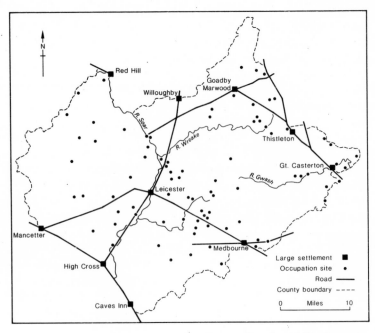

1. Roman Roads and Settlements.

Webster has produced a more elaborate idea of the Fosse Way and its functions. No longer does it seem to be a single-line frontier; instead, the road acted as an axis through the deep defensive zone of forts – a zone in which the river Trent probably played an important part as a means of transport. Again, the problem still remains largely unresolved of whether the Fosse Way began as an original work of Roman engineering, aligned by its military surveyors through the forests of the Midlands. Or was the road perhaps laid down along the path of a prehistoric trackway that had already been in existence for almost 2,000 years?

The remaining important Roman roads of the region all point to the north and the north-west, leading to the capitals of the 'military' zone. Watling Street, now the western boundary of Leicestershire, marches on towards Wroxeter and Chester. Across the open limestone plateau of eastern Rutland, Ermine Street provided a main route to Lincoln, York and the frontier in the north that Hadrian was to establish after A.D.120. Among the minor roads of the Roman period the Gartree Lane, following a course south-eastwards from Leicester to cross the Welland valley beyond Medbourne, is among the most tantalising. In places it is a metalled road today; elsewhere the track degenerates to a footpath whose ancient importance may be suggested by the line of a parish boundary on the Ordnance map. Haverfield, in his classic account of Roman Leicestershire in the *Victoria County History* suggested that the Gartree Road was a minor lane from *Ratae Coritanorum* designed to serve an outlying estate at Medbourne. Now it is believed that the road came into being in the early years of the conquest as a line of military communication between the early Roman base at Colchester and freshly subdued territories in the Midlands. Telling evidence for this view is supplied by the accumulating proof of a Roman fort at Leicester, a fort that may have been manned to legionary strength for a short time.

The study of sites and objects from the Roman centuries in the countryside of Leicestershire and Rutland suggests a society in which native British and alien Roman elements were closely intertwined. Perhaps the most striking conclusion from recent research, largely with the aid of air photography, is the discovery of an enormous number of settlements in the Trent and Welland valleys that seem to have perpetuated their Iron Age characteristics throughout the Roman period.

Three main types of settlement can be identified from air photographs and archaeological finds in the Roman landscape of the East Midlands. There is a handful of places whose original names are known to us because they are recorded in the Antonine Itinerary, one of the rare contemporary sources for the reconstruction of the geography of Roman Britain. Three such places – *Tripontium*, *Venonae* and *Manduessedum* – grew up on Watling Street on the very western border of Leicestershire. *Venonae*, at the crossing of the Fosse Way and Watling Street, seems to have been less important than its position at one of the primary junctions in the communications of Roman Britain would suggest. Recent archaeological investigations at High Cross, at the time of road widening on A5, Watling Street, in the 1950s, failed to reveal the character of *Venonae*. There is proof of continuous occupation of the site from the late first century to the fourth century, but as the report of the excavation records, 'there is no evidence of stone structures or of a military or large scale industrial use of the site throughout its occupation'. The deterministic rules of 20th-century spatial geography would have expected the emergence of a major regional capital at *Venonae*; instead the place where urban life was to flourish stood on the bank of the river Soar at the heart of the present city of Leicester. Another of the minor settlements – possibly posting stations with minor commercial and marketing functions – lay close beside the Fosse Way just across the Leicestershire-Nottinghamshire border at Willoughby on the Wolds. Here too there is the suggestion that a Roman fort was established in the years about A.D.50, but, as at *Venonae*, proof is still wanting. The Roman name of Willoughby on the Wolds, *Vernemetum*, contains a hint that this was a place of importance for the Coritani. The second element seems to be derived from the Celtic word *nemeton*, a sacred grove. Was this already a meeting-place close to a prehistoric road long before the Roman intrusion?

The villa-estate was the most striking and original contribution of the Romans to the countryside of these islands during their four centuries of occupation. In Leicestershire and Rutland a number of villa sites have come to light through the discovery of fragments of building

*Detail from the
Blackfriars
Pavement*

material – pottery, coin hoards, roof and flue tiles, plaster, stone walls and evidence of mosaic floors have all provided clues to the Roman presence. But there are hardly any sites that can stand comparison with the elaborate building complexes that once formed the heart of big estates in the Cotswolds or at the foot of the Sussex Downs. Only one villa, discovered in the 18th century on the west bank of the Soar and now lost to view in suburban Victorian Leicester, matched the largest and most elaborate villas of Roman Britain. For the rest, most of the sites seem to have been simple aisled halls, the homes perhaps of moderately prosperous Coritanian farmers. Such simple estate houses are known at Great Casterton on the banks of the Gwash in Rutland, at Medbourne beside the Gartree Road in the wide vale of the Welland and at Sapcote not far from the Fosse Way in what must have been the heavily forested landscape of west Leicestershire.

Perhaps the most striking conclusion from recent research on life in the East Midland countryside during the Roman centuries is the belief that British customs and modes of land organisation survived for a long time. As Malcolm Todd has written in his excellent study of *The Coritani*, 'almost all the Coritani were closely connected with the life of the countryside – as landlords, as tenants or *coloni* on estates, or as peasant freeholders . . . the fabric of Celtic society survived the Roman Conquest intact'. Of late, aerial photography has suggested an abundance of peasant settlements on the fertile soils of river terraces along the Trent and Welland and in the valleys of the Soar and Wreake. For instance, one of the most fascinating revelations of the recent intensive air surveys is a peasant village of a score of circular huts, most within ditched enclosures, lying on either side of a long droveway at Lockington, close to the confluence of the Trent and Soar in north Leicestershire. This village site awaits excavation, but surface finds already suggest that it was occupied as late as the second century A.D. Less than half a mile to the east is a small villa. Speculation from this slender evidence has led to the idea that here was a village of serfs whose labour was employed on the villa estate. On the other hand, a deeper archaeological investigation may show that at Lockington an Iron Age village was already in existence when the Roman legions took over the East Midlands and that an active community survived until at least A.D. 200. The nearby villa-site may only represent the adoption of some features of a Roman style of life by the British head of a Coritanian estate.

During the Roman centuries the rich lands along the chief river valleys and on the lighter soils of the marlstone and limestone uplands were not only used for stock-rearing and grain growing; there is also considerable evidence for the quarrying of building stone and the extraction of iron ore. Several places in Rutland and north-east Leicestershire have yielded proof of iron smelting. There was a smelting hearth within the walls of the little Roman town of Great Casterton. In the woods above the long-deserted site of the medieval village of Pickworth a group of three shaft furnaces dating from the early years of the second century

24

has been discovered. And it has been suggested that the poorly explored Roman settlement at Market Overton was probably associated with the iron industry. Nowhere in Leicestershire or Rutland can one point to a particular quarry of Roman origin, but it is evident from the recognition of Ketton stone in Roman building at St Albans and at Roman sites in Cambridgeshire that the quarries of the East Midland countryside were already active. Similarly the slates of Charnwood Forest found not only a local market in the nearby regional capital, *Ratae Coritanorum*, but are known from as far afield as Ancaster in Lincolnshire.

The making of a regional capital on the east bank of the Soar was the greatest and most original achievement of the Romans in Leicestershire and Rutland. In the past few years research within the city has established beyond doubt that the Roman town began as a fort laid out beside or within the limits of an Iron Age settlement. What the earliest pre-Roman settlement at Leicester was like remains beyond the grasp of evidence resting only on fragments of pottery and a handful of Coritanian coins. The name by which the Romans knew this tribal capital was *Ratae Coritanorum*, meaning 'the bulwarks, or defences, of the Coritani'. Is there perhaps a long-vanished Iron Age fort beneath the present city?

The laying-out of a planned town at Leicester was going on in the years about A.D.100. The most striking visible survival of the Roman town in the topography of the present city is the Jewry Wall, a ragged piece of masonry that rears up close beside the Saxon church of St Nicholas. Antiquarians, from the great Stukeley in the 18th century onwards, have been attracted by the sight of the Jewry Wall. In the '50s and '60s of this century, archaeologists, frequently in frenzied rescue digs connected with the redevelopment of the city centre, have revealed much more about the Roman town, but alas there is little for the eye to see. The site of the baths, excavated under the direction of Dr. Kathleen Kenyon before the Second World War, is beautifully preserved for all to see beside the Jewry Wall Museum, a model display of a town's earliest history. For the rest, the site of the forum, until recently a mystery in the minds of Leicester's local historians, has now been located as a result of extensive clearance and new road construction around St Nicholas. Unfortunately, heavy stone robbing by later generations and limited possibilities of further excavation mean that the planning of the forum will never been unravelled. But Leicester's importance as a Roman town in the Midlands stands out clearly from all the evidence now gathered. A large number of mosaics as well as a first-century wall painting speak of costly private houses. A market hall, discovered to the north of the forum, was built at the close of the second century A.D. over the foundations of a fine earlier house. As in all active urban communities changes of function and rebuilding were part of a town's development. In Leicester those changes have gone on down the centuries. The growth of a thriving medieval town that later evolved into a prosperous Victorian city has obliterated much of the Roman past so that only the sparsest fragments of the first street plan are known by archaeologists. Only in the last few years has research uncovered the first firm proof of the location of the wall of the Roman town.

Archway in the Jewry Wall

25

IV Anglo-Saxon Colonisation and the Making of Mercia

Iron spearhead and arrowhead, late sixth century, Empingham

Much happened during the seven centuries of Saxon England. A barbarous, pagan northern people evolved into an important focus of western Christendom. The Saxons have been credited with the great task of extensively clearing the primeval forests of Britain, of founding thousands of closely-knit village settlements, of establishing communal systems of open-field farming around their villages. Parishes and counties, the units through which the life of England has been ordered down the succeeding centuries, were carved out during the Saxon centuries. Towards the close of this long period the outlines of the urban geography of the Middle Ages can be clearly discerned.

Until recently it has seemed reasonable to ascribe to the fifth-century settlers from Teutonic Europe the successful task of laying the foundation of the English landscape as we know it today. But lately new views on the meaning of the early Anglo-Saxon place-names for settlement history, a vastly increased knowledge of Saxon pottery, together with new evidence from pagan burial grounds have all contributed to a reinterpretation of the history of the critical fifth and sixth centuries. No longer is this period described as a time of complete break with the Romano-British past when an alien, pagan northern people made a fresh start in the exploitation of the environment of these islands. Now the life of Roman Britain seems to melt, over several decades, into the new mould of Anglo-Saxon Britain. It has been shown that the migration from northern Europe to Britain began at least half a century before the withdrawal of Roman rule from these islands with the settlement of mercenary soldiers, *foederati*, at the outskirts of such important Roman towns as York and Canterbury. It was once believed that the Roman road system fell into disuse within a generation of the abandonment of Britain in A.D.410; now it seems highly likely that the network of Roman roads guided the settlement of incoming Angles and Saxons until the early years of the sixth century. And now it is becoming clear that some of the Roman towns were not abandoned completely.

There is now much evidence that the intrusion of the Angles into Leicestershire and Rutland is different in certain aspects from what was believed 50 years ago when W.G. Hoskins, a pioneer of studies in English local history, presented an important paper on the Anglian and Scandi-

26

2. Anglo-Saxon pagan cemeteries, early place-names, and Roman Leicestershire.

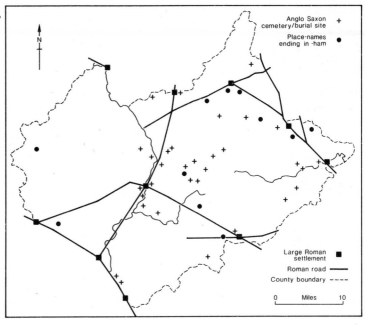

navian settlement of Leicestershire to the Leicestershire Archaeological Society. Then it seemed evident that the Anglo-Saxon colonisation of the heavily forested claylands of the Midlands, remote from the first landings and primary settlements of England's east coast, must have come late in time. Hoskins believed that the first Anglian settlers appeared in the Soar valley about the middle of the sixth century. He wrote of the decades of the abandonment of Britain after the Romans, 'Not until the first half of the sixth century, and probably nearer 550 than 500, can we pick up the threads of history again in this part of the country. From 550 the Angles settled in and colonised the district now known as Leicestershire, slowly and in very localised groups at first . . .'. It was also believed that they found themselves in a totally unreclaimed forest wilderness, and that the founding of villages and hamlets on patches of sand and gravel amid the hostile boulder clays was the prime achievement of the sixth century by the tribe of the Middle Angles.

Recently research on the coming of the Anglo-Saxons into the East Midlands has veered to the view that the pagan intruders from across the North Sea reached parts of Leicestershire and the limestone country of eastern Rutland in the first half of the fifth century and perhaps even earlier, in the closing decades of the Roman control of Britain. The early settlement of the Anglo-Saxons in this region and the location of these first colonists rests upon the evidence of pagan burial grounds and a new interpretation of the chronology of key elements, *-ham*, *-ingham*, and *-ing*, in the primary place-names.

Saxon sculpture, Breedon-on-the-Hill

27

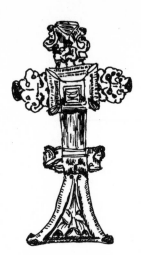

Sixth-century bronze brooch from a pagan cemetery at Empingham

The most striking feature in the pattern of distribution of the cemeteries is their close relationship to Roman roads and Romano-British settlements. For instance, early Anglo-Saxon burial sites have been discovered close to the walls of Roman Leicester at the East Gate and at Westcotes. Not far from the city, and close to Roman roads, cemeteries have been uncovered at Oadby, Thurmaston, Glen Parva and Rowley Fields. The pagan burial sites, dating from before the conversion of the Anglo-Saxons to Christianity at the end of the sixth century, are recognised by the worldly goods that accompanied the inhumations – swords and spears, javelins, shields, brooches and beaded necklaces as well as the urns of the earliest decades when cremation was the usual custom. The cemetery at Thurmaston provides sure evidence of the early presence of the Anglo-Saxons in the Soar valley. Ninety-six cremation urns have been recovered there, dating from the closing years of the fourth century and the beginning of the fifth century. They suggest that the earliest Teutonic migrants were settled close to Leicester well before the Roman withdrawal from Britain. These were probably soldier mercenaries, the *foederati*, whose services were rewarded by the land that they farmed. Similar burial grounds yielding archaeological evidence of inhumations within the Roman period are known at Caistor-by-Norwich and at York.

The pagan cemeteries of Rutland are all confined to the eastern parts of the county, at Market Overton, Cottesmore and North Luffenham. At the beginning of this century when R.A. Smith wrote his chapter on Anglo-Saxon remains for the first volume of the *Victoria County History of Rutland*, he noted the coincidence of the burial grounds with the narrow outcrop of the Northampton Sands, an exposure that never reaches more than a mile in width. He thought of the Saxons as pioneer colonists in a trackless primitive woodland, and ascribed the choice of the Northampton Sands for the location of the first settlements to their light soils, the abundance of springs in these porous rocks, and the dry, healthy sites provided by this gentle escarpment above the marshes, quagmires and tangled woodland of the Vale of Catmose. But if we consider the pattern of Anglo-Saxon burial grounds in Rutland against the known elements of the Romano-British landscape, we see that the cemeteries lie close to the main Roman roads of the county. Ermine Street has provided a major line of communication across the low limestone plateau of eastern Rutland for almost two thousand years. A branch of Ermine Street, the Sewstern Lane, leads north-westward through an important tract of Romano-British settlement around Market Overton and Thistleton. As in Leicestershire the first Anglian settlements seem to have taken root in areas that already formed important nodes of population and economic development in the territories of the Coritani. Again, in Rutland the early date of the first settlements has been confirmed by finds from the cemeteries. The North Luffenham burial ground, used over a period from about A.D.400 to the end of the sixth century, has yielded metal buckles and harness equipment, associated with the soldier mercenaries of the closing years of the Roman occupation.

28

Research in the 1960s has shown that one of the oldest elements among the place-names of Anglo-Saxon England is the suffix -ham, meaning a village, a settlement, a collection of dwellings. The -ham names belong to the pagan period of early English history, to the span of time between A.D.400 and 650. The genuine -ham names of Rutland include Clipsham, Greetham, Langham and Luffenham. On the wolds of East Leicestershire we find Waltham, Wymondham and Wycomb. The early recorded forms of the latter place-name reveal a -ham element that has become transmuted and concealed down the centuries. It has been argued that the first part of this name may derive from the Latin *vicus*, a civil settlement of Roman Britain. Wycomb lies in a belt of rich ironstone country to the north of Melton Mowbray and in the vicinity are the sites of two Anglo-Saxon cemeteries. Is it not possible that the -ham at Wycomb began as a community of Teutonic mercenaries settled in north-east Leicestershire to guard and perhaps provide labour in this Roman iron-ore field before the close of the fourth century?

The -ham place-names of Leicestershire and Rutland seem to show a close relationship to the roads, settlements and occupied places of the Roman landscape. For instance, Wymondham, on the limestone upland of north-east Leicestershire, was established in the fields of a Roman villa estate and lies close to a road that was in use in prehistoric and Roman times, the Sewstern Lane. The same relationship to Roman roads and Romano-British sites seems to govern the distribution of the -ham names in Rutland. Clipsham lies only a mile to the east of Ermine Street. Early Saxon pottery has been found there as well as the characteristic metal work associated with the *foederati*. In the vicinity there is the site of a Roman villa, the remains of iron smelting furnaces of Roman times have been found close by at Pickworth, and the stone quarries of Clipsham are known to have been worked in Roman times. The evidence gained from the study of the distribution of the -ham names is that the earliest Teutonic settlers of Leicestershire and Rutland moved into districts that were already populated, cleared of much of their primitive woodland and served by roads. In Rutland the original Anglo-Saxon settlements lay in the east of the county closely related to Ermine Street. The first settlements in Leicestershire were on the north-eastern wolds, in a countryside crossed by the Fosse Way and a branch road through the iron-ore field to the Sewstern Lane. Much of West Leicestershire seems to have been a wilderness, but the presence of Higham on the Hill, Measham and Goatham suggests islands of early settlement in relation to Watling Street and the Roman tracks that threaded a densely wooded landscape to the west of Charnwood Forest. In fact, it has been suggested that these lonely -ham sites of West Leicestershire were a deliberate creation of late Roman times 'with the express purpose of the policing of the routes by federate settlers'.

A later phase of expansion that began towards the end of the pagan period seems to be indicated by the place-names containing the -ingham and -ing elements. As a general rule the Early English place-names that contain these elements seem to have no close relationship to the Roman

Cremation urn, Thurmaston

29

road system. In both Leicestershire and Rutland their pattern of distribution points to the colonisation of virgin territory, the making of clearings in natural woodland. In Rutland, two of the names with *-ingham, -ingas* elements are Uppingham and Whissendine. Both lie towards the western border of the marlstone country, much of which remained in forest until long after the Norman Conquest. Similarly the later *-ingham* and *-ing* elements in the Leicestershire place-names are found in areas remote from the Roman roads and the vicinity of the regional capital, in the claylands of High Leicestershire and the south-western parts of the country. They include Skeffington, Loddington, Tur Langton and Horninghold in the uplands between the Welland and the Soar tributaries. To the south we find Kilworth, Saddington and Theddingworth.

When the new political geography of Anglo-Saxon England began to take shape in the sixth century with the creation of a number of different kingdoms, the East Midlands fell largely into the huge territory of Mercia. The core of Mercia stretched from the flanks of the Midland plateau, westward of Birmingham, to the Wash, and from the Nene valley to within sight of the hills of the Peak District. But at the height of its power, in the latter part of the eighth century under King Offa, Mercian hegemony reached northwards to draw an uncertain frontier with Northumbria between the Ribble and the Humber and westwards into the Welsh Marches where the greatest earthwork and visible frontier since the construction of Hadrian's Wall, Offa's Dyke, was raised between the Severn estuary and the mouth of the Dee.

Leicestershire and Rutland formed part of the core of Mercia from the beginning, but the details of that beginning are one of the most obscure pieces of Anglo-Saxon history. Orthodox accounts of the making of the Anglo-Saxon kingdoms have always given a late date for the founding of Mercia. This Midland state, it is believed, originated in the first quarter of the seventh century under the rule of Penda with its capital at Tamworth. Recent research on the origins of Mercia suggests that the beginnings of the kingdom reach back to the last quarter of the sixth century, to a line of kings that began with Crida in the year A.D.585. The same piece of research, using evidence from the 12th-century chroniclers, Roger of Wendover and Matthew Paris, contends that the settlement of the Angles that gave rise to the Mercian kingdom goes back to the year 515. Both the chroniclers describe how 'the pagans came from Germany and occupied East Anglia . . . some of whom invaded Mercia and fought many battles with the British; but, since their leaders were many, their names are missing'. If this account of an important episode in early sixth-century history is correct, it means that the East Midlands were occupied either from East Anglia or by closely related Angles from their Teutonic homeland across the North Sea.

The details of relations between the incoming Angles, the founders of the new kingdom of Mercia, and the inhabitants of the former territories of the Coritani remain completely obscure. What is clear, when recorded history sheds a little light on a dark epoch, is the importance of this region in the geography of Mercia. In 679 the territorial arrangements for the government of the church in Mercia were reorganised. The huge see of Lichfield was split up and Leicester became the bishopric of the Middle Angles. Leicester's bishops watched over an extensive territory in the south-east Midlands, extending to the valley of the upper Thames, as the power and influence of Mercia reached its climax in the eighth century. The last king of all Mercia, Burgred, was driven out before the raiding Vikings in 874, and it is believed that the plunder raids of the Northmen resulted in the destruction of almost all monastic records and of the archives that must have formed part of the royal administration at Tamworth. All that remains of this period of greatness at Leicester is a list of the names of bishops. In 737 Torthelm was bishop of Leicester when prayers were said for St Boniface, Eadberht attended a church council in 781 and Waerenberht, who is on record as bishop there in 803 and 814, described himself as 'the bishop of the Middle Angles' and again as 'the bishop of the town of Leicester'. The last in the line of the Mercian bishops of Leicester was Ceolred. He witnessed charters in 843 and 844 and the last time that his name appears is in 872.

The Danish conquest of the East Midlands was complete by 877. Of the time of Mercia's greatness before the destruction of the northern raiders so little has survived. The site of Leicester's first cathedral is not known with any certainty. The most likely seat of the bishops between 679 and 872 was a church on the site of St Nicholas, at the heart of the earlier Roman town and beside the city's oldest market place, at the junction of High Street and High Cross Street. It is not impossible that the stones of the present church, particularly in its north wall, formed part of that cathedral of Dark Age Mercia. Again, it has been suggested that the shape of Mercian Leicester may be descried on the first plans of the city and its streets made towards the end of the 16th century. A crude plan of the city, drawn about 1600, shows the streets of central Leicester about the 'Hye Crosse', contained within a curving oval-shaped lane – all inside the rectangular circuit of the town wall that had been raised over the foundations of the Roman wall. Was this perhaps the shape of the Mercian cathedral town that grew over and amongst the ruins of Roman Leicester? The important question of whether urban life continued within the walls of the city through the fifth and sixth centuries between the withdrawal of Roman power and the rise of Mercia still remains unanswered. But the early cemeteries close to Leicester and the rare finds, up to now, of early fifth-century pottery hint that the Roman town was not totally extinguished as a settlement site.

Little remains in the countryside of Leicestershire and Rutland of the Mercian period of history. Without doubt the finest memorial is in the medieval church at Breedon-on-the-Hill. This limestone hill in north-west Leicestershire was the site of a Mercian monastery. The traditional date of its foundation is A.D.675 and the community, it has long been believed, perished in the Danish raids at the close of the ninth century. From the Anglo-Saxon monastery a score or more of sculptured stones

Bronze pin, Empingham

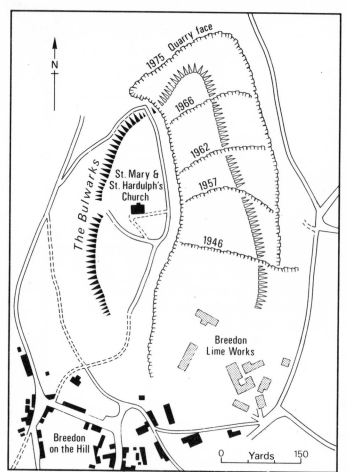

3. At Breedon-on-the-Hill a medieval church, itself on the site of a Saxon monastery, stands within the rampart of an Iron Age camp, the Bulwarks. The greater part of that earthwork has been destroyed since the 1940s by the advancing quarry-face of the Breedon Lime Works.

Celtic goddess, Braunston

remain, most of them now cemented into the walls of the medieval church. Friezes with plant scrolls, animals and abstract ornament, panels with strange quadrupeds and representations of human beings with deep drilled eyes make up this fragment of early Christianity that has survived, almost miraculously, into the 20th century. At Braunston, in Rutland, there remains an even stranger and more mysterious relic of the Dark Ages, or more ancient times. Outside the church stands a crude, powerfully-shaped stone figure, a Celtic goddess. Does she recall a pagan, pre-Christian place of worship among the forests of the marlstone country on the borders of Rutland and Leicestershire where the colonising Angles came late and settled sparsely?

32

9. Bawdon Castle — one of the several farms in Charnwood Forest created by the carving up of the common waste after the Enclosure Act of 1808.

10. Bringhurst — an early 13th-century church on the summit of a low hill that rises from the valley floor of the Welland. The shape and layout of this village — the farmsteads gathered in a shallow circular hollow around the raised churchyard — suggests that an older earthwork, possibly a ring-fort of Iron Age date, preceded the Anglo-Saxon settlement that came to be known as 'the clearing of Bryni's people'.

11. Rutland Water is almost the size of Windermere and is the largest man-made lake in Britain. Started in 1970, it was completed in the year of the great drought (1976). Built to serve the needs of planned urban expansion in the East Midlands at Peterborough, Northampton, Corby, Wellingborough and Daventry, it has been argued that the deep economic recession of the 1980s has rendered the drowning of so much of Rutland superfluous. Nevertheless Rutland has gained a tourist attraction of immense value.

12. Pastoral East Leicestershire — a landscape of deserted village sites where tree-lined hedgerows record the enclosures of the 18th century that erased the medieval pattern of open fields. In the distance, Billesdon Coplow, the one prominent feature of a quiet subdued landscape.

13. Great Stretton — the site of a deserted village, extinguished in the 16th century. As the place-name says, this is 'the settlement beside a Roman road'. The 'street' is the Gartree Road. The lonely little church of St Giles, now disused, was restored early in the 19th century.

14. Wistow — the parish church of a settlement deserted early in the 17th century.

15. A packhorse bridge, five feet in width, at Anstey dates from about 1500. It probably marks the line of a medieval trackway from Leicester into Charnwood Forest.

16. At Medbourne a medieval footbridge leads into the raised circular churchyard of St Giles. This circular enclosure of the parish church suggests an ancient site, possibly that of a long-vanished prehistoric 'henge' monument or stone circle.

V The Danelaw

Towards the close of the ninth century the political order of Anglo-Saxon England was violently disturbed by marauding armies from Scandinavia that ranged widely over the Midlands and the east. The *Anglo-Saxon Chronicle* has preserved a glimpse of these years of chaos in its record of 'a great heathen army' that pillaged East Anglia in the year 865. Between 865 and 868 the Northmen widened their field for plunder and tribute to East Mercia. In the winter of 874-5 the raiders established their quarters at Repton on the river Trent. Monasteries, the repositories of rich and beautiful objects in gold and silver and jewellery, formed particular targets for the pagan invaders. The monastery that had been founded at Breedon in 675 within the earthworks of the Iron Age camp was reputedly sacked by the Danish invaders. Although there is no documentary proof of the date and manner of its destruction apart from this old tradition, it is most likely that the destruction of the first monastic community at Breedon came with the marauding Danish army and, perhaps more exactly, at the time when they were stationed at their winter base in Repton only a few miles away.

Saxon carving, Breedon-on-the-Hill

In its record of the year 877 the *Anglo-Saxon Chronicle* sheds some light on the progress of the Danish military occupation of Mercia in a reference that suggests the permanent settlement of the land. 'The Danish army', we read, 'went into the land of the Mercians, and shared out some of it, and gave some to Ceolwulf.' Ceolwulf was the puppet king whom the Danes placed on the Mercian throne. Mercia it seems was divided; large parts of its eastern territories had passed into the hands of the Scandinavians and were open to settlement. Within the next decade, in 886, the losses of territory in Mercia were clearly defined by a treaty that King Alfred concluded with Guthrum, the leader of the Danes, after the Saxons had recaptured London. The Danelaw comprised the greater part of eastern England from East Anglia to North Yorkshire. Across the Midlands the frontier between West Mercia and the territories ceded to the Danes followed for many miles the line of Watling Street. A Roman road, already a part of the landscape for eight centuries, provided a well-defined feature for the reshaping of the political geography of the late Saxon years.

But the independence of the Danelaw proved to be no permanent feature of the political geography of Britain. Danish Mercia was recovered by the English in a military campaign of 917 and 918, a little more than a generation after the conquest by the barbarians from the

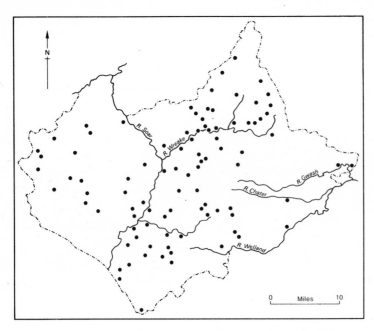

● = place-name ending in -by or -thorpe

north. Nevertheless 40 years of the Danelaw's existence have left an abiding impression on the history of Leicestershire. The ending -by, meaning a farm or more usually a settlement, is encountered by the hundred in the soft landscapes of Denmark. In Leicestershire alone 56 village names end in -by, and of these half the number contain a Danish personal name as their first element. The Scandinavians left an indelible impression on the language of the East Midlands. Vocabulary, grammatical structures and the very tones of local dialect were deeply affected by the contact with Scandinavia. Despite this, the visible remains of the Scandinavians in the landscape are hard to come by. Leicestershire has none of the churchyard crosses with sculptured motifs from the pagan mythology of Scandinavia that we find elsewhere in northern Britain. Burial places, pottery and the implements of everyday life are completely lacking in Leicestershire's archaeological record as signals of the presence of the Danes.

Our understanding of the Danish settlement and the geography of the Danelaw depends largely on the evidence of Scandinavian place-names. Their density and patterns of distribution point to the tracts that must have been settled by Danes in the last quarter of the ninth century. For instance, Welby, Asfordby, Saxelby, Sysonby, Kettleby and Kirby form a cluster of names on the western outskirts of Melton Mowbray. Further along the Wreake we find Frisby, Hoby, Rotherby, Brooksby and Rearsby. But towards Leicester on the broad gravel spreads where the

34

Wreake empties into the Soar, the character of the place-names changes. The sounds of the Scandinavian invader give way to names of an older Mercian origin with endings in *-ton*. Thrussington, Syston, Cossington, Thurmaston – all speak of an earlier period in Leicestershire's settlement history. Even though the *-ton* element suggests the presence of a settlement that survived the impact of the Danish army, the first element in these names is frequently a Scandinavian personal name. The hint is given, though far from proven, that at Thrussington and Thurmaston we are in the presence of the takeover of a Mercian estate by a Scandinavian overlord.

A survey of the place-names of the Soar valley to the north of Leicester shows that the dominant forms relate to the earlier centuries of the Anglo-Saxons. The assumption goes that the corridor of the Soar with its broad and fertile terraces raised above the frequently flooded river flats formed one of the earliest cores of settlement in Leicestershire. There was no land here for the incoming Danes, so they turned towards the emptier and perhaps less rewarding river terraces that flank the narrower valley of the Wreake. The pattern of place-names of English and Scandinavian origin in the Leicestershire landscape presents some baffling problems to the modern investigator. In the Wreake valley, for instance, there is a decided thinning of Scandinavian names towards the river's source where Melton itself marks a much older English settlement. Here, even the name of the river is changed for the headwaters of the Wreake bear the name of Eye, from the Old English *ea*, meaning 'river'. River names of Scandinavian origin are not common in the countryside of England. One wonders what events in the history of Leicestershire towards the close of the ninth century brought about the renaming of the Eye between Melton Mowbray and its confluence with the Soar. The new Scandinavian name, Wreake, seems to derive from an Old Norse word meaning 'twisted'. Professor Ekwall, in his study of *English River Names*, proposed that the name Wreake was a direct description of the narrow, twisting stream that the Danish settlers found in the marshy, frequently flooded floor of this valley.

Silver pennies from the Leicester mint

Sir Frank Stenton believed that the large number of Scandinavian place-names in the Wreake valley indicated the strength of Danish settlement there. He contended that this represented the settlement of a large body of the army in, or soon after, the year 877 when the wandering war-bands in the East Midlands took to the permanent occupation of the land. It is likely that we find among the place-names of the middle Wreake valley, below Melton Mowbray, the last surviving evidence of a Danish army unit that was deliberately settled on the land so that it could spring to the defence of Leicester – one of the five boroughs of the Danelaw – if the town were threatened by Saxon invasion from the west.

Professor Keith Cameron in his study *Scandinavian Settlement in the territory of the Five Boroughs* has taken a somewhat different view. He contends that the soldier-colonists of the late 870s represent the first phase of settlement – a phase for which the *Anglo-Saxon Chronicle* provides a shred of written evidence under the year 877, when it records that 'the Danish army went into the land of the Mercians'. Professor Cameron believes that the Scandinavian settlement of the Wreake valley was only achieved over a longer period of time with the slower occupation by farmers for almost half a century. Cameron thinks that much of the Danish settlement was directed, long after the military occupation, to wild, unoccupied land. He writes, 'though some sites in the area east and north-east of Leicester may well represent earlier English settlements taken over by the Danes, the evidence as a whole suggests that the Danes came predominantly as colonisers, occupying new sites'.

Silver penny from the Leicester mint

The evidence for the occupation of Rutland by the Danes, again depending almost entirely on the forms of the county's place-names, is equally difficult of interpretation. Within the boundaries of the Rutland that survived until 1974 there are no Danish names formed with the *-by* element – names that probably belonged to the earliest period of settlement. Of the names ending in *-thorpe* – an indicator of minor secondary colonisation by the Danes – there are only eleven. In the whole county only six place-names contain elements derived from Scandinavian personal names. The territory of the Rutland that we know seems to have been largely avoided by the incoming Danes at the close of the ninth century. Given the location of the shire, deeply embedded within the eastern plain of England that passed over to the Danelaw, one can only conclude that a strongly Anglian tract of Mercia somehow resisted the waves of settlers from across the North Sea. There is no evidence that Rutland maintained its Anglo-Saxon identity through military resistance. It seems as if some forgotten political arrangement led to a drastic reorganisation of the territory of this part of Mercia. Dr Cyril Hart believes that Rutland, before the Scandinavian invasions, formed part of a larger Mercian district that stretched eastward to include parts of present Lincolnshire and the town of Stamford. One clue to Stamford's former links with Rutland lies in the history of the church of St Peter, now destroyed, that began as the daughter of the church of Hambleton, close to the heart of territorial Rutland. How and when did the eastern parts of the county, if such belonged to Rutland more than a thousand years ago, become dismembered? Dr. Charles Phythian-Adams has proposed 'an early date in the Scandinavian period' for the separation of Stamford and Kesteven from Rutland. *Roteland*, he writes, 'emerges into the light of history as a very English district in the midst of Scandinavianized territory'. Rutland's fate at the end of the ninth century seems to be bound up with the Danish interest in Stamford. The Danes chose Stamford as one of the strong-points of the Danelaw; it was one of the five boroughs along with Derby, Leicester, Lincoln and Nottingham, where a new urban settlement was established close beside an existing Mercian town. The strategic importance of Stamford doubtless lay in its position on Ermine Street. Its transfer to the Danish occupied lands of Lincolnshire was probably achieved out of military and political necessity.

36

The creation of the Danelaw made as great an impression on Leicester as in the surrounding countryside. The colonising Danes, soldiers and farmers, turned the Mercian cathedral city into a garrison town. The term *gate*, descended from the Old Norse, *gata*, meaning a street, occurs in a handful of streets at the heart of the city. All in the same part of the town we find Gallowtree Gate, Humberstone Gate, Church Gate, Belgrave Gate and Sanvey Gate. They all lie outside the line of the former Roman and medieval wall, beyond the bounds of the Anglo-Saxon town. In fact, the first four streets converge at the Clock Tower where the High Street passed through the former East Gate out of the walled enclosure of the medieval town. Thus, the presence of the *gata* element in the modern street names of Leicester suggests that the Danes, when they made this place one of the strongpoints of their newly conquered lands, established a new town outside the wall of the little Mercian city. By the early years of the tenth century Leicester must have been a twin-town sharply divided into Anglo-Saxon and Danish quarters.

It is believed that the Scandinavians who settled the East Midlands were soon converted to Christianity, perhaps within a generation of the break-up of the war-bands in the 870s. The chief evidence for this assumption, tenuous as it may be, is the absence of pagan sculpture and burial customs from the Leicestershire countryside. In the borough a Christian church was established in the Danish suburb, probably before the end of the ninth century. St Margaret's stands on that site, and in the present 15th-century church one can still see the grey-white stones of a building that stood there before the Norman Conquest. This fragment of an earlier church is displayed most dramatically through a glass slab set into the floor. That this was indeed a place of worship for the Danish quarter is strengthened by the diocesan arrangements in the Middle Ages. Long after the tenth century the churches within the medieval wall – the parishes of the older Anglo-Saxon town – were attached to the diocese of Lichfield, while St Margaret's belonged to the ecclesiastical capital of the Danelaw, Lincoln.

Early English font,
All Saints, Leicester

VI Leicestershire and Rutland in Domesday Book

Sedilia, St Mary-de-Castro, Leicester

The Domesday Survey, ordered by William the Conqueror and collated in two great volumes by 1086, presents a view of the greater part of England for the two decades that followed the Norman Conquest. The information summarised in the Survey was gathered for the purpose of taxation. It is concerned primarily with the wealth of the land as a basis for fiscal assessment – the productivity of a manor's arable fields, the extent of its meadows and woodland, the water mills where corn was ground, the rivers, lakes and seashores where fish were caught and salt was boiled from sea water.

From the information recorded in Domesday Book, however inaccurate and incomplete it may be in places, 20th-century geographers have been able to reconstruct the outlines of the economic geography of 11th-century England. In Leicestershire, 296 settlements – hamlets, villages and the borough of Leicester itself – are recorded. The territory that had evolved into the county of Rutland by the end of the 12th century has 39 settlements named. The most striking feature of the map of settlement at the time of the great Survey is its very completeness; only a handful of new names were to be added to Leicestershire over the next 900 years. In fact, Domesday Book contains the names of several places, active farming communities, that have since disappeared from the landscape. Thirty-nine of the deserted villages identified by Professor W.G. Hoskins appear among the Domesday folios as populated agricultural settlements. Although some of the places missing from the Domesday roll-call came into existence only in the succeeding centuries (Market Harborough and Coalville, for instance), others that go without mention must have been there at the time when King William's surveyors combed the East Midland countryside. Bringhurst, possibly one of the earliest Anglian settlements of the Welland valley, is not recorded. Hoskins points a finger at the true explanation when he writes, 'in 1086 the village was undoubtedly silently included in the small soke of great Easton'. For some other places there is strong evidence of their early existence despite their absence from Domesday Book. The Leicestershire Survey, taken in Henry I's reign between 1124 and 1129, provides a check for the contents of the earlier survey. Although the later record covers only part of Leicestershire, it names a dozen settlements, missing from the Domesday record, that must have existed in 1086. For instance, they include Lockington, Hemington and Long Whatton, all of which seem to have been gathered under Shepshed in the Domesday folios. As

Saxon carving, Breedon-on-the-Hill

38

Professor F. M. Stenton, one of the great interpreters of the complex material of Domesday Book, wrote, 'Domesday Book, the greatest of all surveys, is no infallible record'.

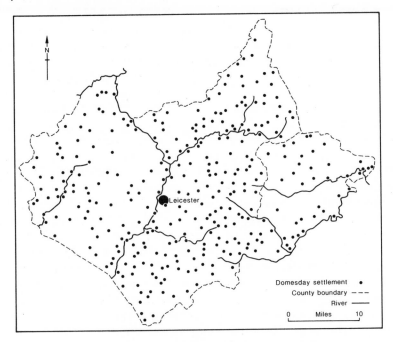

5. Settlements named in Domesday Book.

Domesday Book's laconic statistics tell us nothing about the topography – the buildings, streets, lanes and field patterns – of the 300 and more settlements named in Leicestershire and Rutland. Because its information is set out under the manorial properties of the powerful landowners who swept into England with the Norman Conquest, a village that was divided between several estates will have its resources listed at more than one place. Hose, for instance, in the Vale of Belvoir, was composed of four separate manors, while at Ashby de la Zouch manor and village were coextensive. It was in the possession of one man, Ivo, who was the tenant of Leicestershire's greatest landowner, Hugh de Grantmesnil. The manors of Barrow-on-Soar, Rothley, Great Bowden and Melton Mowbray exhibit an even more unusual structure with scattered holdings in several neighbouring and sometimes distant settlements. Domesday Book tells us that Earl Hugh of Chester was lord of the manor of Barrow-on-Soar, and that he held this estate from the king. Fifteen plough teams worked the land at Barrow and that there were three mills on the river Soar. But this huge scattered property had interests – strips in the arable fields, plough teams and men owing allegiance to Earl Hugh – in 13 other villages. They included close neighbours such as Seagrave and Sileby, more distant settlements such

Saxon window, Norman arch, St Nicholas, Leicester

39

Norman tower of St Nicholas, Leicester

as Gaddesby and the now deserted village of Frisby, lying between Billesdon and Galby. To the west, Barrow-on-Soar had economic ties with Charley, a hamlet in the heart of Charnwood Forest that Domesday Book records as 'waste', as well as Castle Donington.

William and his followers took over an economic and social order that had evolved since the settlement of the Midlands by the Anglo-Saxons. The origin of the four large manors with their several scattered outliers is a matter of much speculation. It has been suggested that they developed in the closing years of the ninth century after the marauding armies of the Scandinavian invaders settled on the land. Danish soldier-farmers occupied land in scattered villages still owing allegiance to warrior lords in the central manors of Rothley, Great Bowden, Barrow-on-Soar and Melton. One important argument in support of this idea is derived from the great number of 'sokemen' recorded in Domesday Book under the large federal or 'discrete' manors. The 'sokemen' were wealthier members of the village population in Norman England. They have been described as 'a peasant aristocracy' and it is believed that they represent the descendants of the Danes who settled the East Midlands in the last quarter of the ninth century. But this is not the only idea about the origin of the federal manors. F.M. Stenton in the first volume of the *Victoria County History of Leicestershire*, noted that the large complex manors of Rothley, Great Bowden, Melton Mowbray and Barrow-on-Soar were royal estates. He believed that as territorial units they were of no great age at the time of the Norman Conquest and that they came into being as 'individual sokemen and groups of sokemen sought the King for purposes of protection . . . and thus became gradually incorporated in a large manorial group while still retaining a measure of economic and tenurial freedom'. Another view of the large, complex royal manor – a problem of origins that belongs to the history of Oakham, another royal manor with five outliers – believes that they are remnants of a much older social order reaching back to Celtic institutions in the pre-Saxon period.

Domesday Book does not give us an absolute total of the population – it was never designed as a census. But people are on record for almost every manor, classified according to their economic and social status. For instance, at Wymeswold, we read that in 1086 there was 'one serf and 11 villeins with four sokemen and four bordars and nine French sergeants have ten ploughs between them all'. The broad categories of medieval rural society are plainly defined, and we are also made aware of those who followed in the wake of the Norman Conquest from Normandy, Brittany and Flanders to settle on English soil. Four Frenchmen had settled at Barkby, while the name of Fulchere Malsor, from the Old French *Malesoevres* (Bad Works), who had 'five oxen in a plough' at Oakham, suggests an unattractive individual whose doings in Rutland were perhaps most unwelcome. The largest settlement in the counties' Domesday record is Bottesford with a total of 120. It is usual to consider the numbers written in Domesday Book as heads of families

40

and important members of the community; consequently students of Domesday have applied a multiplier of five to arrive at a truer estimate of the total population. The recorded population in Domesday Book for the old county of Leicestershire is 6,406, which suggests a total 11th-century population in excess of 30,000. The population on record for Rutland is 1,479 – a grand total of 7,000 that is about equal to the present size of Oakham.

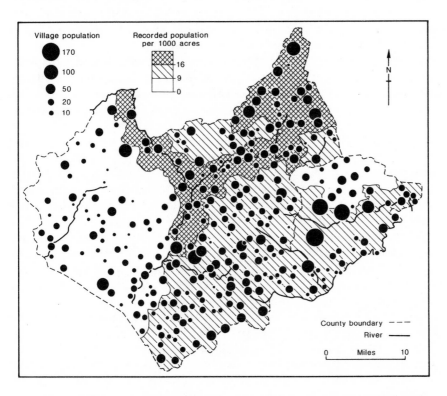

6. The population of Leicestershire and Rutland recorded in Domesday Book.

The countryside of Leicestershire and Rutland in the 11th century can be glimpsed only through an arid collection of Domesday statistics pertaining to ploughlands, plough teams and entries that refer to woodlands and meadows. The meaning of terms *ploughland* and *plough* is far from clear. That they refer to the arable land of each settlement, held either by the lord of the manor, in demesne as the phrase goes, or by the peasantry is evident. But whether this land was cultivated in huge open fields whose scattered strips were owned individually is nowhere made clear in the Domesday folios of any English county. The general belief is that such a system of farming had evolved long before the

41

Norman Conquest. The term *ploughland*, replaced in the areas of strong Scandinavian influence by the word *carucate*, was a measure of the amount of arable land that a plough team was capable of cultivating. The term *plough* seems to indicate the number of plough teams hauled by oxen that worked the arable land. For instance, at Tixover in Rutland, we read that '16 freemen with 4 smallholders have 6 ploughs'. Is it possible from these statistics to arrive at a picture of the distribution and extent of arable land in the two counties in the 11th century? The conclusion of Domesday historians is that the figures for ploughlands and carucates bear no direct connection with the quantity of arable; in the course of time they had become a yardstick for assessment. Plough teams, on the other hand, seem to reflect the distribution of wealth and prosperity throughout the counties in the latter half of the 11th century. Combined with the evidence from the figures of recorded population, it is possible to gain an impression of the settled, cultivated, forest-free tracts of Leicestershire and Rutland.

It is apparent that a marked contrast existed between east and west Leicestershire – the valley of the Soar formed an important boundary in the geography of the county. Donald Holly, in *The Domesday Geography of Leicestershire*, calculated the number of plough teams in 1086 within standard units of 1,000 modern acres. The manors of the western parts of the county average less than two plough teams per 1,000 acres. The Soar valley achieves more than four teams per 1,000 acres and in the eastern parts of the county on the light soils of the middle lias rocks and in the Vale of Belvoir, the recorded plough teams rise to an average of more than five per unit of a 1,000 acres. Holly adopted the same unit of comparison in his study of the population statistics in the Domesday Survey. West Leicestershire's manors never exceed a recorded population of more than seven per 1,000 acres; to the east of the Soar the figure nowhere falls below ten. The most densely populated parts of Leicestershire in the 11th century were the Soar valley, close to the town of Leicester, the rich lowland of the Welland and the Eye Brook on the southern border of the county and the Wreake valley where settlement was focused on Melton. In the most densely populated tracts we find vills with recorded populations of more than forty. Close to Leicester, Whetstone has a Domesday roll of 42, at Oadby there were 59 recorded inhabitants and Wigston Magna produces a total of 86 where the real population must have numbered several hundred. It has been suggested that the settlements close to Leicester had been swelled by the descendants of the Danish armies.

The Domesday geography of Rutland lacks the clear pattern shaped by the Leicestershire statistics. Some of the obscurity derives from the fact that much of Rutland was comprised in the huge federal manors of Hambleton, Oakham and Ridlington. As a result, a score of parish names are missing, their details concealed in the statistics of the large composite manors, amongst them Uppingham, Wardley and Wing, all of which are known to have been in existence before the Norman

Hall of
Oakham Castle

Conquest. Rutland's figures of plough teams and population show the same high returns as east Leicestershire. The eastern fringes of the county, endowed with the light rich soils of the Northampton sands and the jurassic limestones rivalled the population densities of the Vale of Belvoir and the Soar valley in the environs of Leicester.

The entries for woodland among the statistics of Domesday Book provide clues to the less settled countryside where the wilderness survived perhaps from prehistoric times. West Leicestershire, where settlements were smaller and plough teams fewer, was still well wooded in the 11th century. Here, reaching to the North Gate of the borough of Leicester, was *Hereswode* or, as the Domesday entry runs, 'the woodland of the whole Sheriffdom, called Hereswode, has 4 leagues in length and 1 league in width'. The name means 'the wood of the army'; it was probably associated with the Danish army based on Leicester at the turn of the tenth century. Later, as the name Hereswode dropped out of memory, this great tract of medieval woodland became known as Leicester Forest — a name that still passes for the landscape of the M1 to the west of the city. One other important tract of woodland emerges from the statistics of Domesday Book in the south-east of the county straddling the hill country of the Leicestershire-Rutland border northwards from the Welland valley. Until its disafforestation in 1235 this was the Royal Forest of Leicestershire — a territory whose primary purpose was the preservation of wild life for the hunt that found its headquarters at Oakham. An examination of the Domesday woodland figures shows a complete absence of forest in north-east Leicestershire, from the Soar valley to the Lincolnshire border. It is tempting to assume that this area had been completely cleared of its woodland cover in the centuries before the Norman Conquest, but there always creeps into the mind some doubt about the consistency of the evidence of Domesday Book. Did some unknown collector make an incomplete return for this group of Leicestershire manors?

Among the 300 and more places recorded in Domesday Book Leicester stands out as the only urban community. The only other hint of trade and commerce appears in the manor of Melton, held by Geoffrey de Wirce, where we read that there was 'a market which pays twenty shillings'. And we are told that the lord of the manor had granted a tenth of the market tolls to the Abbey of St Nicholas at Angers in Normandy. At Leicester the Domesday statistics reveal, however dimly, the outline of a busy medieval borough. We are told that there were 322 houses in the town in 1086, of which only four are recorded as 'waste' — presumably empty, dilapidated properties, unfit objects for assessment and taxation. Leicester's status as a borough is evident from the mention of 65 burgesses as well as 'moneyers' who rendered £20 yearly. The presence of a mint provides a strong sign that Leicester enjoyed the status of a borough. Domesday suggests that there was a flourishing town of some 2,000 inhabitants on the east bank of the Soar. Most of the life of Leicester must have been gathered within the 130 acres enclosed by the line of the ancient Roman wall. But there was a suburb outside the wall to the north-east, most likely a Danish foundation from the closing years of the ninth century that had been planted by the older Saxon town. This part of the borough may be suggested in Domesday Book's reference to the properties of the Bishop of Lincoln who held '10 carucates of land in the town' as well as '20 acres of meadow, and 3 villeins, a priest and 12 bordars with 4 ploughs' . . . 'outside the wall'. The scene at the end of the 11th century can be gleaned from Domesday Book. The castle goes without mention, although one is confident that the huge castle mound beside the Soar, its original height reaching 40 feet above the river, had been raised by 1086. All that is recorded of the topography of this medieval borough is the mention of six churches. In the absence of specific dedications one must conclude that the main city churches were already the focus of worshipping Christians at the time of the Norman Conquest – the present cathedral St Martin's, St Nicholas, All Saints' and St Margaret's – the latter outside the town wall, to the east, on the estates of the bishop of Lincoln. The two remaining unnamed Domesday churches are probably St Michael's and St Clement's – parishes that had vanished before the Reformation.

Motte and bailey of Hallaton's Norman castle

44

VII Medieval Leicester

The face of Leicester in the 20th century is largely that of a Victorian town. The years of rapid growth in the 19th century obliterated many topographical features of what had been the most important medieval town, after Coventry, of the English Midlands. Domesday Book, with its record of 322 houses and 65 burgesses, suggests that the inhabitants of Leicester numbered no more than 2,000 at the end of the 11th century. Three hundred years later, the Poll Tax Return of 1377 shows that there were 2,000 tax payers in Leicester, a figure that hints at a total population of about three thousand. For almost two centuries there is little evidence of further growth. At the close of Elizabeth I's reign Leicester counted about 3,500 inhabitants and it is only in the following decades between 1600 and 1670 that the urban population rose to 5,000 – a figure calculated from the Hearth Tax Returns with their list of 1,024 households in Leicester.

The Norman Great Hall of Leicester Castle

The modest population of medieval Leicester was largely confined to the 100 or so acres enclosed by the wall that had been raised over the foundations of the Roman defences. Even within the bounds of the medieval wall a considerable amount of space was given over to gardens and orchards. Two important thoroughfares crossed in the heart of the town. The Welford Road marked part of the route from London into the north Midlands. It passed through the town by Highcross Street, between the South and the North Gates. Close beside St Nicholas churchyard a crossroad with the Fosse Way determined the site of Leicester's oldest market place. The two main roads linking the four gates of the walled town divided the enclosed space into four quadrants occupied by seven parishes. Seven parish churches suggests a substantial urban population, one whose true total may be somewhat greater than that obtained from the projection of statistics contained in medieval tax returns. The sites of the medieval churches in Leicester provide a clue to the distribution of population in the town. Only two parishes, St Martin's and St Mary de Castro, lie south of the road axis between the West Bridge and the East Gate. The northern quadrants of the town contained St Nicholas, All Saints and the three lost parishes of St Peter's, St Clement's and St Michael's, all of which had disappeared by the end of the 16th century.

During the medieval centuries it seems likely that the northern segment of Leicester, especially the parts adjacent to the main road leading to the North Gate, was the busiest and most densely populated part of the town. There is further evidence, gleaned mainly from the

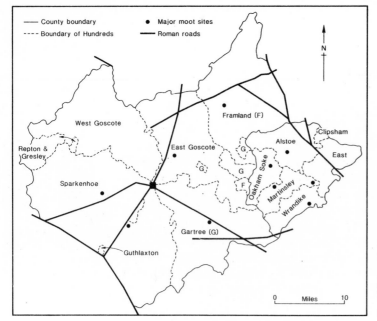

N

West Goscote

Framland (F)

Repton & Gresley

East Goscote

Clipsham

Alstoe

G

East

Sparkenhoe

G

G

G

F

Oakham Soke

Martinsley

Wrandike

Gartree (G)

Guthlaxton

0   Miles   10

7. The medieval hundreds of Leicestershire and Rutland with their moot sites. The proximity of the hundred meeting-places of Gartree, Guthlaxton, Sparkenhoe, East Goscote and Framland to former Roman roads suggests that these ancient routes still played an important part in the county's communications in the Middle Ages.

medieval records of the borough, that life centred in the northern and western quarters of the town. There were several public buildings in this district – the earliest guildhall and its successor, known as the Mayor's Hall, that stood in Blue Boar Lane in St Nicholas parish, the gaol, St John's Hospital and the Shire Hall all lay within a stone's throw of All Saints church. This also was the industrial quarter of medieval Leicester. The tiny parishes, cramped within the line of the town wall, that were already in being at the time of the Domesday Survey, have been used by Professor Geoffrey Martin as evidence for the presence of 'a substantial mercantile community late in the Old English period'. He believes that some of the parishes must have come into being as a result of church endowments by rich merchants in the years before 1143 when the control of the town's churches, except for St Margaret's lying outside the wall, passed completely into the hands of Leicester Abbey.

The industries of medieval Leicester provide further evidence of the concentration of the life of the borough in the northern quarters. Cloth manufacture, bell-founding, leather-working and dealings in wool were the main commercial interests of the burgesses. The wares of Leicester's clothiers were purchased by royalty and an exemption from the tax on cloth, granted in 1202, suggests that the borough ranked fourth among the English textile towns, occupying a place as important as North-ampton's or Winchester's. There is much evidence to show that this industry was located in streets close to the river in the northern part of the town. Deeds from the early 13th century show that the fullers lived in the vicinity of the North Gate, outside the town wall, in a lane that stretched from Highcross Street towards the river. Until the beginning of the 15th century it was known as Walkers Lane, but soon after 1417, with the cloth industry almost extinct, the present name of the street, Soar Lane, had come into use. Research by M.P. Dare in the borough records has shown that there were nine tanneries and five footwear manufacturers at the beginning of the 14th century, and a list of shop rents from 1376 names 13 shoemakers. The tanneries lay close to the river in the district of the North Gate and it is likely that this part of the town attracted the tanners not only because of a plentiful supply of water for the vats from the Soar but also on account of the need for oak bark from Leicester Forest that here reached almost to the wall.

The 15th-century tower of St Margaret's, Churchgate, Leicester

Why did the northern quarters of Leicester fall into decline at the end of the Middle Ages? Three parishes had disappeared by the 16th century – a symptom of poverty and falling population. Until the factories of Victorian industrialists occupied much of this district after the middle of the 19th century, much of the land to the north of the High Street had been taken up with gardens and orchards. C.J. Billson, in his *Medieval Leicester*, believed that the emptiness of the northern quarters until late in the borough's history could be explained by the disastrous events of 1173, known as the Leicestershire War, when the earl of Leicester rebelled against the king, Henry II, and the town was besieged and burnt. The argument goes that the northern quarters of the town were ruined, much of the population fled the city, never to return, the parishes of St Michael and St Clement became depopulated soon afterwards and land was given over to orchards until the arrival of industry in the 19th century. The facts of Leicester's economic history speak strongly against this explanation. Long after the sack of Leicester the industrial heart of the medieval borough was centred here. The explanation of its decline seems to lie in the changing economy of the town after the 14th century. Cloth manufacture was no longer of any importance; instead, the borough became deeply engaged in the wool trade to export markets that lay in the industrial towns of Flanders. Perhaps her most eminent citizens, and some of the wealthiest, from any period of Leicester's history may be found in the closing decades of the Middle Ages. Roger Wigston was Lieutenant of the Staple at Calais in 1483, and at a later date William Wigston the Younger was mayor of Calais. He died in 1536 when the fortunes of the Wigston family were at their height, for a taxation survey made a dozen years before his death showed that William Wigston alone owned 22 per cent of the taxable property in Leicester. His wealth left its imprint on the topography of the borough in the foundation of Wyggeston's Hospital.

Much of Leicester's medieval 'townscape' was erased in the succeeding centuries; even so, ample visible evidence still survives from the period between the Norman Conquest and Henry VIII's dissolution of the

47

monasteries to allow the vigilant explorer of the city's streets to recall the chief elements of that lost medieval society. The castle mound, raised beside the Soar close to the south-west angle of the Roman city wall, is the only evident relic of the Norman Conquest and the earls of Leicester who managed their extensive scattered estates in the Honor of Leicester from this stronghold. It seems most likely that the building of Leicester's fortress was part of the Norman conquest of the Midlands in 1068 when castles were raised at Nottingham, Warwick, Lincoln, Huntingdon and Cambridge. Some of the town castles are mentioned in the Domesday record; for instance, we are told that houses were cleared at Lincoln to make way for the castle and its bailey. What happened at Leicester is not known. Its position within the perimeter of the Anglo-Saxon town, not far from the Wednesday market and the site of the cathedral before the Danish conquest of the Midlands, suggests that this might have been a built-up part of the town in the 11th century. Again, there is some evidence of a church in this quarter before the founding of St Mary de Castro. But it has also been argued by Peter Liddle, in a recent survey of the archaeology of Anglo-Saxon Leicester, that a belt of empty land, formerly occupied by fortifications of late Saxon and Danish date, lay inside the south wall of the town and that the castle, the Saturday market, and the Franciscan friary occupied this gap in the urban pattern.

The 12th century was an important period in the making of medieval Leicester. Within the castle bailey, to the north of the palisaded motte, Robert le Bossu built the hall; with its timbered roof this building has been described as 'the oldest surviving aisled and bay-divided hall in Europe'. Although the Hunchback's hall still stands, the renovations and alterations of subsequent centuries have destroyed the splendour of the original building. Since the end of the 13th century the castle's hall has been used as an assize court. In 1690, the east wall was pulled down and rebuilt in brick and in 1821 an even more drastic renovation saw the interior divided into two courts and several other rooms. Today, if one wants to enjoy the interior of a 12th-century castle hall one must journey to Oakham.

An equally important part of the life and landscape of medieval Leicester was the abbey, founded among the meadows of the Soar beyond the north wall of the borough by Robert le Bossu in 1143. When Henry VIII destroyed the monasteries, Leicester Abbey was the second wealthiest of the Augustinian houses in England. Over the centuries the abbey had accumulated properties in many parts of the Midlands – granges in the Peak District with their valuable harvests of wool, estates in Leicestershire that included the acres of deserted Ingarsby, and the patronage of scores of churches. In Leicester, where the abbey's properties were not extensive, the monks' chief holding was the manor of Bronkinsthorpe to the west of the river. Records show that Leicester's merchants provided the chief outlet for the abbey's wool; for instance, in 1297-8 Hugh le Mercer, an important Leicester wool-trader, was

Remains of tower, Leicester Abbey

48

17. West Bridge over the river Soar, Leicester.

18. Leicester Castle — the timber-framed Gatehouse, built in the 1450s.

19. Hallaton — among the most attractive of South Leicestershire's villages. The Green with its circular, conical-shaped market cross recalls a once busy medieval centre where the Poll Tax Return of 1381 records not only farmers but carpenters, tailors, weavers, cobblers, a wheelwright, a baker and a brewer. The parish church of St Michael has one of Leicestershire's finest broach spires.

20. Fragments of medieval Leicester survived the great rebuilding of the Georgian and Victorian decades. One of the finest is Wyggeston House where behind a late 18th century brick front an early 16th-century timber range with an oversailing upper has escaped destruction. The building is now the Leicester Costume Museum.

21. Burley-on-the-Hill — John Lumley's Burley House, built for the Second Earl of Nottingham between 1694 and 1705, ranks among the greatest of the mansions of the English aristocracy. A principal feature of the vast enclosing park, where Repton worked, is the Avenue — the viewpoint in this photograph.

22. Latimer House, Thurcaston — a timber-framed L-shaped farmhouse that was probably built in two stages in the 15th and 16th centuries. The oldest part of the building was the birthplace of Hugh Latimer, Bishop of Worcester, born 1470 and burnt at the stake, a Protestant martyr, in 1555. In a sermon preached before King Edward VI Bishop Latimer mentioned his birthplace, 'my father was a yeoman, and had no land of his own, only he had a farm of three or four pounds by the year and hereupon he tilled so much as kept half a dozen men'.

23. Leicestershire's churchyards preserve a rich collection of finely engraved headstones in Swithland slate. The earliest examples of this local art date to the 1760s, the last to the 1860s.

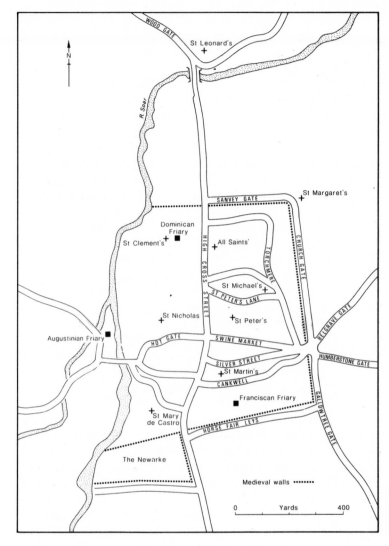

8. The main streets of medieval Leicester showing the sites of the lost churches of St Peter, St Michael and St Clement.

buying extensively from the abbey. Scarcely anything remains of this great monastery and its material riches. The outline of its church is marked by stones in Abbey Park. There is some original work in the boundary walls and an excavation of the 1920s turned up a number of 14th- and 15th-century tiles.

Another splendid piece of the medieval townscape has all but vanished from a site adjacent to the south wall of the borough where in 1330 Henry of Lancaster, earl of Leicester, founded the Newarke Hospital. In 1355, his son Henry, created duke of Lancaster in 1351, enlarged the area of the Newarke and established there a college of secular canons.

49

The Magazine Gate

The magnificent scheme of the Newarke was three generations in the making. The College of Leicester was one among half a dozen late medieval foundations that included St George's, Windsor. The most striking survival of the Newarke, apart from its commemoration among the street names of Leicester, is the Magazine Gate, the original entrance to the walled precinct of this medieval college. The name 'Magazine' recalls a later phase of national history when the Newarke gatehouse was used as a magazine for storing arms in the Civil War.

The greatest loss among the buildings of medieval Leicester after the abbey church must be 'St Mary's of the New Work', a name given to the collegiate church to distinguish it from the neighbouring St Mary de Castro. All that remains today of this church are fragments in the basement of the polytechnic. Yet, by the end of the 15th century, it must have ranked among the finest of the Midland churches, reflecting the commercial and political importance of the borough. Here were the monumental tombs of the College's founder, Henry, first Duke of Lancaster; John of Gaunt's Spanish wife, Constance; Mary, Countess of Derby and first wife of King Henry IV. The Lady Chapel sheltered the monuments of the Shirley family and in the north aisle of the nave three of Leicester's merchant princes, the Wyggestons, lay buried. As Professor Jack Simmons has written in *Leicester – Past and Present*, 'princes of the blood, the peerage, the gentry, rich and public-spirited merchants – 'the whole hierarchy of the English governing class is represented here, within the walls of this one building. It was a building that Leland, Henry VIII's perceptive topographer, described not long before its destruction as "not very great, but it is exceeding fair" '.

The life of medieval Leicester was dominated by the castle and those who administered its affairs on behalf of the earls of Leicester. The borough and its institutions evolved out of the long relationship between Leicester's citizens and their magnate overlords. Simon de Montfort, whom the city commemorates in street names, public buildings and monuments, exercised his unfettered power in the borough through acts that changed the laws of inheritance and banished Jews from the town 'on the grounds of their usurious oppression of the inhabitants'. Despite Leicester's unique political role among the leading English towns, where the authority of the earl eclipsed that of the king, the medieval centuries witnessed the slow development of the power of her burgesses. Borough institutions were shaped out of the relations between the earls, their stewards, and the burgesses. It was from the relationship between the castle and the trading community that the government of the borough evolved. In 1118 Count Robert of Meulan made the grant of a guild charter to 'his merchants of Leicester'. It paid respect to customs of the merchant community that looked back to the time of William the Conqueror, a hint that there was organised trading in Leicester from before the Norman Conquest. By 1196, the year of the earliest surviving Guild Merchant Roll, we find that 50 different occupations are recorded among its members. If the beginnings of civic government in Leicester are connected with the rise of a merchant community, they are equally associated with a medieval court, the Portmanmoot, that came into being for the settlement of minor disputes. By 1199 the Portmanmoot had become a court of record for conveyances of property, but there is the belief that this body, composed of 24 members known as the Jurati, two bailiffs and a clerk, originated with the Danish occupation of Leicester at the turn of the ninth century. From the middle of the 13th century the presiding officer of the Portmanmoot and the guild were closely bound with each other in the management of the affairs of Leicester and in the intermittent bargaining with the castle. As Mary Bateson has written in her close analysis of the medieval records of the borough of Leicester, 'both Guild and Moot are municipal organs and both give birth to the Town Council'.

By the end of the 15th century, the ancient bodies, Portmanmoot and Guild Merchant, which had regulated the life of Leicester, gave way to a single centralised institution which presently came to be called the Corporation. An outstanding landmark of the growth of local government through the medieval centuries in Leicester is the Guildhall, the meeting place of the Corpus Christi Guild, that was built in 1390 close beside St Martin's church, now the Cathedral of Leicester. A century later, by the 1490s, the Corpus Christi Guildhall was used for the meetings of the governing body of the town. Its remarkable survival, a timbered medieval building in the heart of a Victorian city, is owing to its use as a town hall until the latter half of the 19th century when the new town hall was built in the 1870s.

14th-century Guildhall, Leicester

VIII The Making of a Medieval Landscape

The three centuries that followed the Norman Conquest mark one of the most vital periods in the making of the English landscape. There is much evidence to show that it was a time of rising population, a population whose demands for living space were to leave a considerable impression upon the countryside. The sum total of Leicestershire's medieval population – a Leicestershire contained within its old boundaries before the recent engorgement of Rutland – may be discerned through the statistics of Domesday Book and the Poll Tax Returns of 1377. Domesday Book suggests that the grand total of the county's inhabitants in 1086 lay between 25,000 and 30,000. The Poll Tax Returns, a record of all adults over the age of 14 upon whom a tax of fourpence per head was levied, show that there were 31,730 such individuals in Leicestershire. In his study of *British Medieval Population*, J.C. Russell calculated that the total population of the county at that time was 47,595. But Russell has also argued that the effects of the Black Death must be remembered when we look at the figures of the Poll Tax Returns. Between 1348 and 1377 the Plague had visited this part of the East Midlands four times. It is probable that before the appearance of the Black Death, in 1348, the population of Leicestershire had stood at about 60,000. In the centuries after the Norman Conquest the population more than doubled.

The simple pattern of growing population revealed by two historic sources three centuries apart in time becomes somewhat confused when the skills of local historians are applied to the evidence from individual villages. A survey of villages in part of Leicestershire survives from the year 1279. It was transcribed by the early 17th-century antiquary William Burton, and part of it is printed by Nichols in his classic topography of the county. A comparison of the information contained in this 13th-century survey with that of Domesday Book made by Professor R.H. Hilton suggests an overall striking increase in population. The numbers are almost doubled. But some places seem to have remained uncommonly stable. For instance, Domesday Book shows that Market Bosworth had seven sokemen and 25 slaves, villagers and smallholders. Almost 300 years later, in the Village Survey, there are seven free tenants – a status similar to that of sokemen – and 25 villagers. At Mowsley, among the attractive hills in the south of Leicestershire, the figures in the two accounts suggest a strikingly different population history between the Norman Conquest and the last quarter of the 13th century. Mowsley is a late Saxon settlement from the evidence of the place-name. *-Leah*, meaning a woodland clearing, enters late among the place-names of Anglo Saxon settlement history, and Ekwall in his *Dictionary of English Place-Names* explains it as 'the mouse-infested clearing'. Domesday Book suggests it was a tiny settlement of '1 serf, 5 villagers and 2 smallholders', still lost perhaps in deep, primeval woodland. In the 13th-century Village Survey Mowsley enters simply with 35 free tenants. Not only is there a hint that the population of Mowsley quadrupled over the two centuries since the Domesday Survey, but also that a remarkable change in its social structure had taken place.

The contrasting figures of population growth in Market Bosworth and Mowsley lead one to speculate on the causes behind these different demographic patterns. Does Mowsley's growing population over almost three centuries represent the natural increase of a tiny settlement, or was this semi-wilderness the object of colonisation from the long-settled parts of the county? On the other hand, the static condition of Market Bosworth's population suggests that here was a place with a steady out-migration to the remnants of wilderness in west Leicestershire.

The woodland statistics in Domesday Book reveal extensive areas of forest in west Leicestershire and in the hilly tract on the borders of the county with Rutland. In addition, belts of timber, scrub and natural waste existed on the boundaries of manors where room was available for the expansion of the open fields around old settlements. Medieval records, increasingly abundant from the beginning of the 13th century, show that a steady encroachment was taking place in the remnants of Leicestershire's wilderness. For instance, at Swannington, on the western fringe of Charnwood, a wide stretch of moor and woodland was available for cultivation. A record from 1293 shows that a local jury testified that it was lawful for each freeman of Swannington 'to take land in from the waste and cultivate it according to the size of his existing holding'. Not all improvements of the wilderness were achieved without opposition. Only seven years earlier, in the neighbouring village of Thringstone, Alan of Thringstone was accused by the prioress of Gracedieu of inclosing 80 acres of wood. As a result, the destruction of Alan's inclosure was ordered. The same kind of evidence for the taming of the wild comes from places in the east of the county. At Skeffington the abbot of Croxton was accused of inclosing and ploughing-up 80 acres of moor.

The retreating frontier of wilderness over the three centuries since the Norman Conquest may be traced in some features of the East Midland countryside that have survived into our own times. Place-names, especially those of individual fields, tell of patches of land freshly cleared from woodland. The term *assart* is common in medieval documents. It means to clear woodland through the grubbing up of trees and bushes to make way for arable cultivation. Among the field-names of Leicestershire, we find Prestgrave Sart, while the record of a 13th-century grant of land in Quorndon refers to '128 acres of assart land'. In some places the expanding population moved beyond the confines of the parent

53

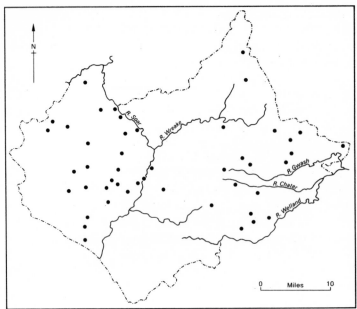

9. Medieval parks — a distribution pattern that reveals the wildest parts of Leicestershire's landscape in the late Middle Ages.

settlement to establish an isolated farm or nascent hamlet in the more distant woodland. Such medieval colonisation, mainly in the 13th century, is written into the present topography of the south-western fringe of Charnwood Forest. The place-name elements *-hay*, *-hayes*, and *-haw*, all derived from the Old English *haga* meaning a 'hedged enclosure', belong to woodland settlements of the post-Domesday expansion. Today, on the outskirts of Ratby where the M1 cuts a deep swath across the flank of Charnwood, we find a landscape of medieval colonisation. From the old villages of Groby and Ratby, founded long before the Norman Conquest, new farms had been cleared a mile and more out in the rim of enveloping woodland. We recognise them today by the names Old Hays and Bondman Hays close against the parish boundary between Ratby and Thornton. At Old Hays an 18th-century farmhouse still stands within the moat that must have been dug when the original settlement was made almost 800 years ago. Another of the medieval clearings in Charnwood's ungrateful wilderness, Alderman's Haw, was owing to the efforts of a monastery. The Cluniacs of Bermondsey established a cell here early in the 13th century. A record, dated 1278, tells of its existence, but 100 years later there is no further trace of this monastic retreat. Only a place-name tells of the original clearing.

Although the pattern of medieval expansion largely took the shape of new strips added to existing open fields, patches of waste taken into cultivation, and lonely farms lost in woodland, more rarely a fresh

Old Hays,
Ratby

54

settlement came into being. Newtown Linford is such a place. The very name suggests its origin, a new 'ton' – a fresh settlement in the eyes of someone at some time in history. Fortunately there is sufficient evidence to pinpoint in time the appearance of this village whose name means 'the new hamlet at the ford by the lime trees'. It probably originated as a daughter settlement of Groby in the latter part of the 13th century. Domesday Book tells us that Groby was already in existence in 1086. In 1288 a reference to Groby mentions rents drawn from new assarts. A few years later the farmers of Groby are on record as holding 165 acres of assart at Newton. The making of a hamlet at Newtown Linford towards the close of the 13th century is thus established beyond doubt. This straggling village at the entrance to Bradgate Park still recalls something of its beginnings in a medieval woodland clearing. The shape of the village, a half-mile-long straggling succession of cottages along a lane – some of them preserving cruck-framed structures – is typical of pioneer settlements in woodland. Still more telling are the strips of ridge-and-furrow that run back from either side of the main street. Today, they are best viewed to the north of the village from the steep overlooking slope of Bradgate Park.

The landscape of Leicestershire bears a visible legacy from the decades that followed the Norman occupation – a legacy of castles, churches and monastic buildings. Altogether Leicestershire and Rutland possess some 20 castle-sites dating from the years of the Norman occupation, and the period of anarchy and civil war in the 12th century associated with Stephen and Matilda. In addition there are earthworks, at Thorpe Arnold and Ridlington, that have been ascribed to the Iron Age but which might well belong to the century of castle-building after 1066. Apart from the huge castle mound that was raised beside the Soar within the walls of Leicester and the magnificent hall at Oakham, one of the best examples of a Norman motte and bailey occupies the gentle slope of the shallow valley above Hallaton. The site, low down almost in the valley floor, suggests that strategic and defensive functions played little part in the location of this castle. Hallaton seems to have been the centre of a compact estate owned by Geoffrey Alselin, a Norman magnate named in Domesday Book. Archaeological excavation at many of these lonely castle mounds ought to reveal much more of their history. Hallaton Castle was subject to excavation a century ago at the time of the building of the railway that is now as much a landscape fossil as the Norman castle. A railway engineer made it his spare-time occupation to dig within the bailey. He turned up ample proof of a living community there in the form of pottery, leather shoes, wooden bowls, together with evidence of iron-working in the bailey. But an investigation of the castle mound at Groby by Brian Davison in the 1960s provided even more intriguing revelations of the age of castle-building in the 12th century. The motte contains the core of a pre-existing stone building whose walls ranged between two and five metres in height. Its purpose is not clear, but Davison suggests that it is either the stronghold of an earlier lord, or even the foundations of a church tower from the Saxon period.

Tower,
Ulverscroft
Priory

The decades that followed the Norman Conquest saw the rebuilding of many churches, the foundation of some of England's greatest cathedrals, and a rich flowering of monasticism – a movement that drew much of its material strength from the gift of estates, urban properties and bundles of strips in the open fields of many manors. Of church rebuilding in the 12th century there is much evidence in both Rutland and Leicestershire. Tixover's massive grey Norman tower, the magnificently ornate chancel arch in the little church at Tickencote and the west front of Ketton speak plainly of the church's power in these times, even in Rutland which has no great medieval cathedral. By the end of the 12th century half a dozen Augustinian monasteries had either been founded or re-established by the Norman aristocracy. Breedon, on a flat-topped limestone hill close to the northern border of the county, overlooks the wide vale of the Trent. The site is exciting – a former Saxon minster within the rampart of an Iron Age camp that passed to the Augustinian Order early in the 12th century. The present parish church at Breedon consists of the chancel of the priory church that was rebuilt in the 13th century. Most complete among the monastic remains of Leicestershire and Rutland is undoubtedly Ulverscroft, an Augustinian priory founded in 1134 in a secluded valley in the heart of Charnwood Forest. There are the extensive ruins of the priory church, the prior's lodging surviving as a private house, as well as medieval walls, ditches and fishponds. Fishponds, a regular element in the topography of monastic sites, may be also seen at Launde, Owston Priory where the chancel of the monastic church still provides a place of worship for the parish, and at Brooke Priory in Rutland. Visible remains of a handful of monasteries have disappeared completely, only to be recovered by the patient work of archaeologists in this century. The ground plan of Croxton Abbey was recovered in the 1920s in an excavation organised by the duke of Rutland. Garendon Abbey, the only Cistercian house in the county, was obliterated when the Phillipps family built Garendon Hall at the close of the 17th century. The house, empty since World War II, was demolished in 1965 and over the subsequent six years the Loughborough Archaeological Society uncovered the foundations of the Chapter House and the east end of the church. It is noteworthy that, apart from the great foundation on the northern edge of the county town, the religious communities took up land in the scarce remnants of wilderness in this well-populated East Midland countryside – in Charnwood Forest and in the wooded borderland of the two counties where we find Launde, Owston and Brooke priories.

The medieval centuries of expansion in the countryside are reflected in the emergence of markets and the establishment of fairs. By 1350, 44 places in Leicestershire and Rutland are on record with the possession of market rights. All but two of the long list of market charters date from the years after· 1200. Only Melton Mowbray, with a record of market rights dating to 1077 and Belvoir, granted a charter in the first quarter of the 12th century, predate the spate of market charters issued between 1200 and 1350. But it is evident that several of the market places must be much older than the earliest surviving record of a charter. Leicester's earliest grant of markets and fairs belongs to the year 1229, but there is no doubt that the county's capital was busily engaged in trade long before the Norman Conquest. Many places in the list of charters have long ceased to engage in the localised regional patterns of trade that were characteristic of the Middle Ages – one thinks of Gaddesby (charter granted in 1306), Kibworth Beauchamp (1223), Lubenham (1327) and Wymondham (1303). Those forgotten market days and week-long fairs have not passed without some influence on the topography of several East Midland villages. Hallaton clusters around a market square – a green space now with a market cross. At Barrowden, in Rutland, the wide village green with its loose ring of grey, limestone farmhouses was the place of former fairs and markets. Place-names and topography can provide clues to village markets of which we now have no documentary record. There is no proof that the right to hold markets was ever granted to Frisby-on-the-Wreake, but a 14th-century market cross still stands and one of the streets bears the name of Cheap End. The latter place-name derives from the Old English *ceping*, 'a market'.

The list of medieval market charters shows that most of the places had already enjoyed a long history as rural communities, but there is one notable exception, Market Harborough, where the right to hold markets, first granted in 1203, was acquired by a settlement that had been in existence for little more than a generation. There is no mention of Market Harborough in Domesday Book at which time *Hauerberga* – the hill where oats grow – was an outlying part of the fields of the royal manor of Great Bowden. The earliest record of *Hauerberga* as a settlement appears in a Pipe Roll of 1176-7 when the size of its contribution to the royal coffers of seven marks is equal to that of Great Bowden. This suggests that a place of some importance had come into being, an importance that was soon to be rewarded with a market charter. Certain features of Market Harborough's topography still suggest a newly created settlement of the Middle Ages. One notes the long wide market street and the noble church dedicated to St Dionysius, of which the most striking feature is the absence of a graveyard, a visible indication that burials long after the foundation of Market Harborough had to be made at the mother church of the parish in Great Bowden.

The beginnings of villages and towns are so often obscured by the absence of documentary record. The *Hauerberga* that had become *Mercat Heburgh* by the early years of the 14th century is no exception. There is much to suggest that we are in the presence of a newly founded settlement, but the ruined chapel of St Mary-in-Arden, with the evidence of a Norman doorway, suggests the site of an older hamlet in the same part of Great Bowden's fields close to an earlier crossing of the Welland than that made by the Leicester to Northampton road that forms the axis of the new medieval town.

The Butter Cross, Hallaton

57

IX The Late Medieval Centuries

The closing decades of the 14th century have been recognised as a time of radical change in the economic and social history of England. From his research among Leicestershire's medieval statistics, Professor W.G. Hoskins came to the conclusion that the 'Black Death marked a climax in the making of the medieval landscape'. After the middle of the 14th century there is no more evidence for the founding of fresh hamlets and villages. Instead the last 200 years of the medieval period show that more than 60 villages in Leicestershire alone were deserted, some so utterly lost that all trace has disappeared from the landscape.

The effect of the Black Death upon the population of the county is hard to estimate and there is little precise evidence for the rate of demographic recovery from an epidemic of such proportions as that which overwhelmed Britain and western Europe in 1348-9. The plague in fact dominates the social history of England in the middle years of the 14th century for it appeared again in 1361 and 1368-9. Estimates suggest that the Black Death removed between one-third and one-half of the total population. Contemporary records speak movingly, if not quantitatively, of this demographic disaster. For instance, on 4 May 1349, the Bishop of Lincoln dedicated a new churchyard at Great Easton, a village that up to that time had buried its dead in the graveyard of the mother church at Bringhurst, almost a mile away on the summit of a gentle hill above the floor of the Welland. And the Bishop goes on to explain the reason for the new churchyard in the chapel-of-ease at Great Easton. 'There increases among you, as in other places in our diocese, a mortality of men such as has not been seen or heard aforetime from the beginning of the world, so that the old graveyard of your church is not sufficient to receive the bodies of the dead.' In Rutland the deaths of one-quarter of the clergy are recorded in the year 1349. The economic consequences of the plague are equally striking when the survival of a local record briefly illuminates the scene. An inquisition taken at Belvoir in 1353 reports that there are three ploughlands worth only 60 shillings 'on account of the plague and for lack of tenants'. Another survey, made after the death of the lord of the manor of Whitwick in 1427, states that 12 out of 31 holdings have been passed into the lord's hands on account of lack of tenants and that 300 acres of the demesne arable have been

Ruins of
Bradgate House

converted to pasture. But by this time the first onset of the Black Death had happened almost a century earlier. The 15th century is the high period of village desertions. By then it is difficult to weigh the decimation of population caused by the plague against the market forces of the rising demand for wool that made it more profitable for landowners to put down the arable common fields to pasture and to disrupt to the point of extinction the life of village communities.

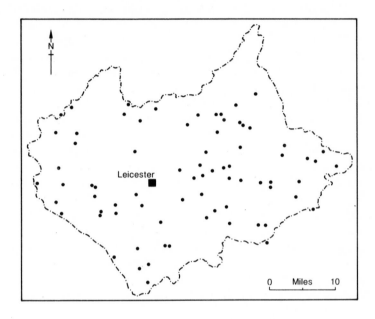

10. Deserted medieval villages.

W.G. Hoskins, in a deeply-researched study of two Leicestershire villages presented in a lecture to the Leicestershire Archaeological Society, reveals the problems and contradictions that beset the student of medieval demography. Galby and Frisby, neighbouring settlements in the gently broken countryside of south-east Leicestershire, seem to have escaped the deep scars of the Black Death in their population statistics. The Poll Tax Return of 1381 lists 73 inhabitants of Galby who were living in 33 households. Three hundred years earlier, Domesday Book suggests that there were 30 families in Galby. There is an increase of only three households over as many centuries. Hoskins believes that the statistically silent years between the Domesday record and the Poll Tax Return saw phases of growing population stabilised by the periodic appearance of great natural catastrophes – the famine of 1315-16 and four onsets of the plague between 1348 and 1375. The most striking decline of Galby's population began in the 15th century. By 1563, when Galby's population was counted for the Bishop of Lincoln, only 14 families worked the land there. Population had fallen by more than one-half since the 1381 Poll Tax. The collapse of Frisby's population began in the second half of the 15th century, almost a century after the first appearance of the Black Death. By Elizabeth I's reign only eight households were left.

The declining rural population of the 15th and 16th centuries revealed in the microcosmic world of Galby and Frisby signals the deep economic and social changes that have left their mark on the landscapes of Leicestershire and Rutland in the sites of some 80 deserted villages. But these East Midland counties represent only a fraction of the desertions that recent research has traced over the greater part of lowland England. The county lists of sites compiled by *The Deserted Medieval Village Research Group* already in 1964 showed a total of 2,263 abandoned villages – places now visible only as a pattern of faintly sunken lanes and the sketchy outlines of house foundations imprinted on green pastures. In Leicestershire the lost villages, 65 all together, form 15 per cent of the total of rural communities that were alive and active at the beginning of the 14th century. Elsewhere the losses were even higher; in Oxfordshire, for instance, 25 per cent of the villages vanished in the late medieval desertions. Until research was concentrated on the numerous deserted sites many went unrecognised and the explanations for the few known abandoned villages amounted to little more than idle guessing. Oliver Cromwell was looked upon as the great destroyer, at Great Stretton and Cold Newton for example. In fact, not one desertion can be ascribed to the civil warfare of the 17th century. Failing Cromwell, early speculation was content to see the Black Death as the chief destroyer. At least this pandemic happened closer in time to the dates of so many desertions revealed by local research. In Leicestershire, 40 of the 65 desertions belong to the late medieval period, to the 15th century and the early years of the 16th century. But the Black Death cannot be claimed as a primary and sole cause of any of Leicestershire's medieval desertions. Studies of individual sites, particularly through the unravelling of their demise through historical records, has revealed the complexity of this problem. But underlying all the changes of the 15th century we find the expansion of sheep rearing to serve the export of wool to the cloth towns of Flanders and Italy as well as the rising textile industries of London, Coventry and East Anglia. The monasteries played an important part in the wool trade and we find that the estates of priories and abbeys were especially liable to desertion.

Ingarsby occupies a high place in the history of Leicestershire's medieval desertions for the clarity of its history and the abundant visual evidence that still remains to be seen on the ground. Professor Maurice Beresford and J.G. Hurst, in their encyclopaedic work on England's deserted villages, indicate Ingarsby as a site that ought to be preserved on account of the quality of its earthworks and the richness of its documentary evidence. The actual day of its destruction in 1469 is known when Ingarsby became 'the Abbot of Leicester's grange'. Over a period

A single arch – all that remains of the village of Pickworth

60

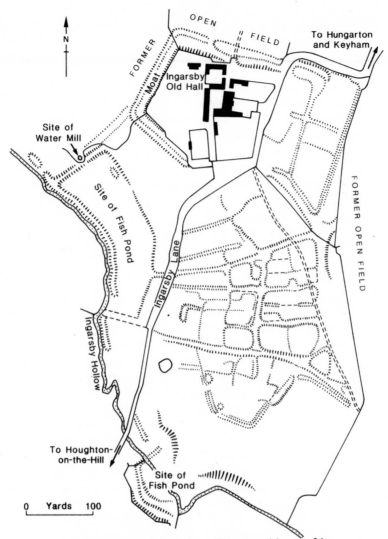

11. The site of Ingarsby still bears evidence of its medieval occupation with hollow lanes, house-plots, earth dams that held up fishponds and the one-time open fields.

of more than a century it is possible to trace the events that led up to the extinction of Ingarsby as a living peasant community. In 1352 a large part of the manor had been granted to Leicester Abbey with the exclusion of a dozen messuages – the land occupied by dwelling houses – and 12 virgates of arable land in the common fields around the village. A quarter of the estate of almost 1,200 acres still lay outside the control of the Abbey, but over the succeeding years the monks acquired complete possession of Ingarsby. For instance, in 1458, nine virgates were purchased from Thomas Ashby of Quenby. This formed the prelude to the desertion, a decade later, of the whole settlement. Today, as we explore the grassy earthworks of Ingarsby on the steep west-facing slope above the brook that drains towards Hamilton, another deserted site, we can pick out clearly features that were imprinted on the land long before that day in 1469 when the monks of Leicester brought about the extinction of the village. A green hollow still marks the line of a village street and slightly raised grass-grown platforms indicate the foundations of farmsteads and cottages – sites that had probably been built and rebuilt many times since the foundation of Ingarsby long before the Norman Conquest. The dimpled chessboard pattern of lanes and crofts gives way, on the flatter hill top above the valley, to the ridge-and-furrow of the once cultivated arable strips in the former open fields. Down in the valley the broken remnants of earth dams locate the sites of fishponds and a large pool that gave a head of water to drive the corn mill.

Ingarsby Old Hall is the only building that remains in this village that sheltered as many as 150 souls at the time of the Domesday Survey. The house dates from the end of the 16th century – a rebuilding by the first squires, the Cave family, who had purchased the manor of Ingarsby from the Crown, in 1540, after the dissolution of the monasteries. But there seems little doubt that the Hall occupies the site of the monastic grange and there is evidence for this in parts of the present building that date from the 15th century. The site of Ingarsby Old Hall, on a spur that divides the shallow valleys of converging brooks, was probably occupied by the manor house of the Daungervills before Leicester Abbey obtained possession of the property in the middle of the 14th century.

Ingarsby's history is a model of clarity among the scores of medieval deserted villages, but even so there is much that remains unexplained in the story of its extinction. Above all, contemporary records provide no clues to the motives that led the abbot of Leicester in 1469 to bring about the extinction of a community of peasant farmers. Was it mere greed – a desire to profit from the growing wool trade? One cannot deny the prosperity of Ingarsby as a monastic grange for in 1535 the valuation of England's monasteries, the *Valor Ecclesiasticus*, showed that it was the richest of Leicester Abbey's properties. On the other hand, it is not impossible that the laying down of the open fields and the conversion to sheep pastures was forced upon the managers of this abbey estate by social and natural events. Almost a century before its final extinction, Ingarsby ranked among the poorest villages in the county. The Poll Tax Return of 1381 mentions only a dozen families. If this figure is trustworthy, the settlement had been reduced to less than half the size recorded in the Domesday Survey. Earlier, in 1334 – before the Black Death – Ingarsby's tax quota of nine shillings was the lowest in the county. Is it possible that the Black Death reduced still further a community in decline so that labour was no longer available to work a large part of the open fields? If much land had fallen out of cultivation towards the end of the 14th century, the way was prepared for its transformation into a sheep farm – an easy task when all lay in the hands of a single owner.

The countryside around Ingarsby is scarred with the sites of several deserted villages. At Quenby and Lowesby, where the Ashbys were lords of the manor, village communities had disappeared by the end of the 15th century. Lowesby had been enclosed and converted to pasture by 1487 and Quenby, which had listed 14 households in the Poll Tax Return of 1377, was reduced to three by the early years of the 16th century. By Henry VIII's time the scale of enclosures and the consequent destruction of close-knit rural communities had become a problem of which even the government had to take notice. In August 1518 a commission to investigate enclosures sat at Leicester and among its evidence preserved in the Exchequer Rolls we find that the Ashbys are cited for enclosure and the conversion of arable land to pasture at Lowesby from 6 February 1487. At Quenby the Ashbys enter the record as landlords as early as the beginning of the 14th century. Late in the 1480s, possibly at the same time as their conversion of Lowesby, they enclosed the open fields of this small medieval village and went over to large-scale sheep farming. But between 1620 and 1630 the landscape of deserted Quenby underwent another transformation at the hands of the Ashby family. The present mansion, Quenby Hall – the finest early 17th-century house in Leicestershire – was built and the park created. Within the same cluster of deserted east Leicestershire villages in which Ingarsby lies we find Baggrave with still a different pattern of dissolution. In its prime Baggrave was composed of a long street of farmsteads on a gentle slope leading down to the Queniborough Brook. Early 14th-century tax assessments show that it housed about 15 families – a total population of less than one hundred. Leicester Abbey owned land here from before the Black Death, but there was no move towards enclosure until 1500 when the abbot converted part of the open arable to pasture. Half the village fell into ruins as five farmhouses and two cottages were pulled down. More land was laid down to pasture in 1501 and 1503 and, although enclosure was now extensive, it seems not to have been complete, for a century later an *Inquisition Post Mortem* shows that this severely shrunken settlement comprised a manor house, four cottages, a dove-house and a water-mill. Although most of the former open fields were under pasture, 660 acres in all, there still remained 20 acres of arable at Baggrave in 1610. Baggrave dwindled towards extinction through the first half of the 17th century; by the time of the Hearth Tax Return of 1666 we find that only the Hall is listed. The countryside where Ingarsby, Baggrave, Lowesby and Quenby lie covers 4,000 acres. By the beginning of Elizabeth I's reign only eight families were left to manage the land that had once been in the hands of 50 households.

Only the stables remain from Martinsthorpe Hall, built on the site of a lost village

The growth of population in the centuries that followed the Norman Conquest made, as we have seen, considerable demands upon the land and its resources. The diminution of woodland and waste meant that these parts of the Leicestershire and Rutland landscape became increasingly valuable for their stocks of wild life, as places where the sport of hunting could be pursued and as sources of ever scarcer supplies of

63

The Bede House,
Lyddington

timber for building, fencing and fuel. Leicester Forest reached almost to the northern wall of the city, but the greatest extent of forest straddled the boundary between Leicestershire and Rutland. The medieval Forest of Rutland occupied half the area of that county. In no sense was this an empty wilderness. The 'Forest' harboured a dozen ancient and thriving settlements. Wright's *History and Antiquities of the County of Rutland*, published in 1684, makes this clear in its description of the by-that-time severely reduced Forest of Rutland 'containing within the said limits the following towns, viz Brook, Braunston, Belton, Wardley, the Mannour of Leigh, Ridlington, Uppingham, Ayston, Stoke, Lidington, Snelston, Caldecot'. Medieval forests, although richly wooded, were legal entities more than distinctive landscapes. Here the Forest Laws applied, laws that were aimed at the preservation of wild life and the promotion of hunting. In theory, though less so in practice, the Forest Laws forbade the building of houses, the taking-in of land for cultivation and the cutting of timber except under strict controls.

Records relating to the management of the Forest of Rutland provide a glimpse of its life and landscape in the medieval centuries. For instance, in the winter of 1222 a great storm swept across the Midlands – doubtless created by the passage of a vigorous Atlantic depression. As a result, Hasculf de Hathelakestun, warden of the Forest of Rutland and Leicestershire, sent out letters to the foresters and verderers (officers of the Crown whose duties were to deal with breaches of the Forest Laws), concerning the disposal of windfall and uprooted trees. Another entry among the records of Rutland Forest for 1232 reveals the use of the woodlands for building materials when Theobald de Bellehus was granted 10 oaks for his manor house at Whissendine. And there was the injunction that the trees were to be taken where they would be least missed. Later, in 1285, the Keeper of Rutland Forest, Ralph Malore, was ordered to supply 12 oaks 'to repair a chamber and chapel in Rockingham Castle'. Towards the close of the 15th century, the name Rutland Forest fell out of use. Its place in the records is taken by Leighfield Forest; Leighfield is now the site of a deserted settlement in the lonely hilly country close to the Leicestershire border. The Verderers' Certificates of the Tudor period throw light on the economy of this waning tract of medieval woodland. By now a hedged boundary had to be maintained to divide the diminishing wilderness from the peasants' fields and the encroaching pastures of greedy, sheep-rearing Tudor squires. We read that the keepers of the Forest of Leighfield 'delivered forty loads of thorns to the fencing of the forest ring of Leighfield and of Ridlington Park'. And once again we see the harshness of winter indelibly imprinted in the records of the Forest with a reference, in 1568, to 'Bowbearer who took, felled and sold wood bruised by the weight of snow'.

24. The High Street, Uppingham — an attractive succession of buildings dating from the 17th and 18th centuries in the rich brown local 'ironstone'.

25. Uppingham — the parish church of St Peter and St Paul is seen from 'the country side'. The original building of Uppingham School, founded by Archdeacon Johnson in 1584, can be seen to the right.

26. Sir Ernest Newton's Hall at Uppingham School with its powerful angle turrets conveys an impression of a Cambridge college rather than a public school in a small Rutland market town.

27. Uppingham School entered a spectacular period of growth with Edward Thring's appointment as headmaster in 1853. By the 1880s the school had 12 houses and its expansion is reflected in a succession of buildings of which The Hall by Sir Ernest Newton dates from 1923–4.

28. and 29. King's Norton — A fine iron gate (*above*) forms the entrance to St John the Baptist at King's Norton; (*below*) one of the earliest churches of the Gothic Revival built for the squire, William Fortrey, by the Leicester architect, the younger *Wing*, between 1757 and 1775.

30. St Nicholas, Leicester — the city's oldest church was probably a cathedral of eighth-century Saxon Mercia. It now serves as the University church.

31. The parish church of St Martin became Leicester's cathedral in 1927 — here seen from New Street.

X Landscapes of Aristocracy

The building of substantial country houses depended upon the disposal of an abundance of wealth – wealth that has rested in the ownership of land for the most part. Consequently one finds that their foundation and their halcyon decades are associated with the titled aristocracy. For instance, Belvoir Castle was founded towards the close of the 11th century by Robert de Todeni, a member of that Norman aristocracy whose strength lay in the numerous Saxon manors taken over at the Conquest. Lord Hastings, builder of fortified houses at Ashby de la Zouch and Kirby Muxloe possessed *Belvori* in the 15th century. Later, in the 1520s, Belvoir passed to the Manners family of Northumberland who as a long line of Dukes of Rutland have been associated with this place until the present day. No trace of the first Norman castle survives. The rebuilding that the first Earl Manners of Rutland began in 1528 was largely destroyed in the Civil War. Between 1654 and 1668 the eighth earl rebuilt Belvoir as a mansion whose solid four-square shape must have resembled the castles at Nottingham and Norwich. And yet again, in the first years of the 19th century, the fifth Duke of Rutland raised the buildings that we know today. Bradgate was founded by Thomas Grey, First Marquis of Dorset, at the close of the 15th century. Staunton Harold, second only to Belvoir as the largest house in Leicestershire, was designed and built by the fifth Earl Ferrers between 1760 and 1778. Stapleford and its park was the province of the Earls of Harborough and the bleak grandeur of Rutland's Burley-on-the-Hill was raised for the Earls of Nottingham.

Belvoir Castle

The distribution of the country houses reveals a clear concentration to the east of the Soar corridor. Although the west contains the oldest visible relics of the dwellings of the aristocracy in Ashby Castle, Kirby Muxloe and Bradgate, the only notable examples of later buildings are Staunton Harold, the Hall at Market Bosworth and Coleorton. One of the most sumptuous of west Leicestershire's mansions, Gopsall, was built by Charles Jennens from a fortune amassed in the Midland iron industry; it was completely demolished in 1952. Garendon Hall, on the outskirts of Loughborough, a fine early Georgian house that was much reworked in the 1860s by Edward Welby Pugin, has also been erased from the landscape, although the scattered remnants of the landscaping of its great park may still be enjoyed.

The sparsity of large, expensive domestic buildings in the western parts of the county reflects, in part, the economic histories of Leicestershire's two contrasted regions. It might be argued that Rutland and eastern Leicestershire were favoured as the sites of aristocratic residences on aesthetic grounds, because of the attractive landscape. Georgian tastes found no pleasure in the rougher qualities of mountain scenery. Perhaps, for similar reasons, the constricted dells and rocky outcrops of Charnwood Forest were rejected. Whatever the taste of the times when some member of the aristocracy came to lavish his wealth on the building of a great house, factors of this kind must have played only a small part in the regional location.

The link between medieval deserted villages and the subsequent building of country houses and the laying out of parks is evident at numerous sites. A village that housed a dozen families in the 14th century has disappeared at Nevill Holt. Its demise probably dates to the time when Thomas Palmer received a royal licence in 1448 to 'impark' 300 acres of arable land. At Nevill Holt, hall and church form a continuous block of buildings, an impressive sight when viewed across the windy pastures of this ridge high above the Welland valley. The buildings of Nevill Holt record the family histories of the Palmers and the Nevills – the latter successors of the medieval manorial lords by marriage. The core of the house, a medieval hall with an open timbered roof, was the work of the Palmers in the 15th century. Much of the rest of the building was done by the Nevills towards the end of the 17th century. The church itself belongs largely to the 13th century. Its very presence here recalls a vanished village community, but the interior with its Nevill tombs in alabaster and black marble remind one of a place of worship transformed into a family mausoleum.

Until the greater internal peace of Tudor times the aristocracy displayed their personal wealth in castles and fortified mansions. There are no remains of Saxon halls or palaces. Of buildings from the medieval centuries Leicestershire and Rutland possess five fine examples. The hall of Oakham Castle, dating from the closing years of the 12th century, is the earliest complete hall of its kind anywhere in England. Here at Oakham a glimpse of the domestic life of the Norman overlord Walkelin de Ferrers has been preserved. At Oakham the columns that separate the central nave from the aisles of the Hall so closely resemble similar work by the mason and architect William de Sens at Canterbury Cathedral that it is assumed that a member of William's professional body of masons went to Rutland to work for Walkelin de Ferrers. Leicester Castle too contains a Norman hall whose roof has been acclaimed as the 'earliest residential timber-roof of Europe'.

The next oldest houses date from the closing years of the 15th century. All three, Bradgate, Ashby Castle and Kirby Muxloe, lie to the west of the Soar. William Lord Hastings obtained the 'licence to crenellate' – a right to fortify his houses. Ashby Castle's building history reaches back to the middle years of the 12th century when the Beaumonts, Earls of Leicester, raised the first hall there. This hall, with much reshaping and rebuilding in the 14th and 16th centuries, stands to the west of the huge grey sandstone tower house, 90 feet tall, that represents William Lord

Hall, Oakham Castle

Hastings' fortifying. The same Lord Hastings who was Edward IV's Lord Chamberlain engaged in an even more striking piece of building on his manor at Kirby Muxloe where on the site of an older moated manor a palatial house in dark red and blue brick was started in 1480. The builders of Kirby Muxloe Castle followed the characteristic plan of the Edwardian castles of Wales. A wide moat encloses an angle-towered wall and gatehouse; inside a large courtyard sheltered the domestic buildings. Unfortunately Kirby Muxloe never reached completion. Under Richard III, William Lord Hastings fell from power and was beheaded in the summer of 1483. The work ceased in the following year and only the gatehouse and the west tower stand to remind one of the oldest building in brick in Leicestershire. All three of these sites remind us that Leicestershire was the scene of much military action during the Wars of the Roses, apart from, of course, the decisive battle of Bosworth.

Tower,
Kirby Muxloe

Henry VIII's dissolution of the monasteries and the enrichment of Tudor England's aristocracy and rising squirearchy contributes another element to the history of the country house in Leicestershire. Grace Dieu, an Augustinian priory founded in 1240 on the northern fringe of Charnwood Forest, became the residence of John Beaumont at the time of the disbanding of the religious orders in 1539. By the end of the 17th century, Sir Ambrose Phillipps demolished most of the buildings at Grace Dieu. What remains forms one of the most picturesque monastic ruins in Leicestershire. Later still, in 1833, the Phillipps of Garendon were to build a new house at Grace Dieu.

The sites of deserted villages, monastic estates that had passed into secular hands, and the opportunities provided by the enclosure movement for the individual development of the landscape form the background to the building of country houses in Leicestershire and Rutland from the early years of the 17th century to the time of Queen Victoria. The developing society that emerged from the upheavals of the Tudor century was severely shaken by the need to take sides in the Civil War. At the beginning of the conflict, the southern part of Leicestershire, including Leicester itself, was held for Parliament by Lord Grey of Groby, assisted by Sir Arthur Hesilrige; but the northern part was under the control of the royalist Henry Hastings, second son of Lord Huntingdon. The rivalry between the Hastings and the Greys went back to the mid-16th century; both sought to obtain dominance within the county. Leicestershire's geographical position meant that rival armies were constantly passing through it, as in 1643 when one royalist force under Queen Henrietta Maria held a rendezvous with another at Ashby de la Zouch. Both Leicestershire and Rutland suffered from the depredations of garrisons, the houses of gentry and noblemen which were now held as strongpoints for one side or the other. They received some of their funding from their high command, but, especially in the case of the royalists, this source was irregular and generally insufficient for their needs. They tended, therefore, to levy what they required from the surrounding countryside.

Grace Dieu
Nunnery

There were five garrisons in Leicestershire alone, and one in Rutland,

67

Burley House

at Burley House. The castle at Ashby was held by Henry Hastings for three years, and eventually, when the victory of parliament was undeniable, Hastings was allowed to surrender honourably and marched out with full military honours. Parliamentarian Burley was not so fortunate; after the siege of Leicester in 1645, when resistance was clearly useless, the garrison evacuated and destroyed the mansion themselves.

Leicester had been staunchly parliamentarian throughout the war. Charles's forces, moving north from their former headquarters at Oxford, called on the commander, Colonel Sir Robert Pye, to surrender, but in vain. After extremely fierce fighting, in which the royalists 'lost three to one', they succeeded in forcing their way into the town. The war had been going badly for them for some time, and the stout resistance of the Leicester garrison seems to have the last straw. Not only were the parliamentarian soldiers beaten and abused, but many civilians as well, a fact admitted by the royalist historian Lord Clarendon: 'the conquerors pursued their advantage with the usual license of rapine and plunder, and miserably sacked the whole town'. The surrounding countryside also seems to have suffered severely at the hands of the royalists, so that one parliamentarian eyewitness thought, 'the losses will not be repaired there seven years'. One result of the siege is said to have been the conversion of the irreligious John Bunyan after a friend took his place as sentinel on the walls of the city one night, and was shot dead by a royalist sniper. The abuses of the royalists brought their own retribution, however. They had lost men in the siege, and now lost more when soldiers deserted with their plunder. These factors contributed to the decisive defeat which the royalists suffered in June 1645, barely a month after the siege of Leicester, near the village of Naseby.

The physical destruction wrought by the war was not its only legacy. Many Leicestershire and Rutland families lost fathers and sons, though few, one hopes, on the scale of George Bathurst of Theddingworth, who lost six sons in the royalist cause. One of the strangest memorials of the Civil War is the church founded by Sir Robert Shirley, an ardent royalist, in his park at Staunton Harold in 1653, a time when, as an inscription reminds visitors, 'all things sacred were throughout ye nation either demollisht or profaned Sir Richard Shirley Barronet founded this Church whose singular praise it is to have done ye best things in ye worst times and hoped them in the most callamitous. The righteous shall be had in everlasting remembrance'. Shirley was constantly involving himself in plots to overthrow the government, and was eventually captured and imprisoned in the Tower, where he died, aged only 28, in 1656. The Cave family provide a sterling example of loyalty rewarded; John Cave, rector of Pickwell, was so notoriously faithful to the king that he was fired at by parliamentary soldiers whilst preaching in his pulpit. His son lived to become chaplain to Charles II.

Stanford Hall, on Leicestershire's south-western border with Northamptonshire, Withcote, Lowesby and Baggrave Halls carry the mind through the early decades of the 18th century. Then comes Staunton Harold, a grand Palladian house of warm red brick and creamy limestone, started in the 1760s around an early 17th-century building. In Rutland the evidence of the building of great houses and even palaces is all around us. The early 17th century is represented by Hambleton Old Hall and the picturesque ruin of the Old Hall in Exton Park – a house that was burnt down in 1810 – which was built by the Noels, Viscounts Campden, Earls of Gainsborough. Lyndon and South Luffenham mark the transition to the 18th century. From this time Burley-on-the-Hill in its vast park overshadows all rivals. The site of this 'palace' endows it with a dominance over the surrounding landscape that can only be matched at Belvoir Castle.

Rutland, for its size, has more than its share of lost houses. Martinsthorpe, in the hilly country of the western border with Leicestershire, was deserted at a date unknown towards the end of the 15th century. In 1622 the pastures of Martinsthorpe passed, by marriage, into the hands of the Earl of Denbigh, who built a country seat there. By the 1750s the house had been sold to the Duke of Devonshire who ordered the demolition of the buildings in 1775. Only the stables, converted to a farmhouse, were left standing for the shepherd who tended the pastures that had long before taken over the arable strips of Martinsthorpe's open fields. Normanton, Rutland's greatest loss, was pulled down after the Second World War. Some of its stones were carted to Scraptoft, on the outskirts of Leicester, to be used in another building. An even greater threat to the landscape of Normanton came with the construction of Rutland Water in the 1970s. Britain's largest man-made lake, completed in 1976, has all but engulfed the Baroque church. Normanton is a typical estate chapel, a town church in the country. Now this memory of a vanished social order stands out from the southern shore of Rutland Water.

The most palatial of aristocratic houses were built in the 18th and 19th centuries and in this same period the deepest impressions were made on the landscape. The parks around their houses were transformed into landscapes determined by aesthetic principles. At Exton, Burley-on-the-Hill, Garendon and Staunton Harold landscaping on a grand scale with artificial lakes, long avenues, planted spinneys in harmonious eye-catching locations, decorative summer houses, and follies can be seen. Several of the smaller houses, such as Wistow, Baggrave or Gumley where the house has been demolished, all illustrate in miniature the same principles of aesthetic land management. But the most striking memorial to the rich and titled in the landscapes of Leicestershire and Rutland lies in the parish churches associated with the big estates. Bottesford and Exton crammed with the tombs of the Earls of Rutland and the Noels form a permanent expression of those decades of power. The tombs at Bottesford range through eight Earls of Rutland. But many a parish church commemorates with greater modesty the families that dominated the life of Leicestershire and Rutland until the 20th century. Among such simple examples of the lord and his landscape one likes to remember the Wigleys of Scraptoft where James Wigley, who died in 1765, is commemorated by a monument showing Mr. Wigley engaged in tree-planting.

*Normanton
church tower*

*Bottesford
monument*

69

XI The Landscape of Enclosure

Quebec House

The different components of the English countryside – lanes, hedgerows, footpaths, the quilted pattern of fields – each has its own history. As the primeval wilderness of Leicestershire and Rutland receded at the hand of many generations of farmers, so the landscape and all its features assumed a man-made aspect. Today, as we explore this East Midland countryside, everywhere one is impressed by the visual impact of the enclosures that obliterated the open fields of the medieval village communities. Often the time of this radical change is recorded in the names of new brick-built farms raised among the former open-field strips at the heart of the compact holdings that took the place of the once scattered acres. Sileby, a parish in the Soar valley below Leicester, possessed open fields on the higher spurs of the wolds to the east of the village. The lane from Sileby to its neighbouring village, Seagrave, is surrounded by large substantial farms, lying a quarter and a half miles from the road, with names like Quebec and Belle Isle. Close by Belle Isle, across a brook that drains to the Soar, lies Hanover Lodge. The history of the middle years of the 18th century is remembered in the names of these farms – the time of Hanoverian George II, of the Seven Years' War with France. At the same time profound changes were afoot in Sileby for in 1758 a Parliamentary Act of Enclosure sanctioned the reorganisation of farming there with the blocking together of the scattered strips in the open fields into compact holdings. The Award, the document that detailed the nature of the enclosure, followed on 30 June 1760.

The first of Leicestershire's Parliamentary Acts of Enclosure was passed in 1730 for the parish of Horninghold. All the evidence for Horninghold's enclosure suggests that this was no more than a legal recognition of what had already happened. There the open fields had already vanished in the first quarter of the 17th century. Enclosure Acts for places in Leicestershire tumbled one after another through the parliaments of the reigns of George II and George III. Twelve enclosure awards were drawn up in the 1750s and the year 1760 saw the passage of 11 acts through parliament. The busiest decade for the lawyers and appointed enclosure commissioners was the 1760s with acts covering 41 places in the county. The last bastion of open-field farming, Medbourne, fell to the enclosers in 1842.

There is abundant evidence that enclosure of parts of the communal fields had been going on for a long time before this process was recognised and recorded in the acts of 18th-century parliaments. In 1599 Francis

Haslewood of Belton was 'accused of labouring by all ways and means to induce the tenants and farmers of Belton to inclose fields and convert to pasture'. Again, from Barleythorpe a letter, written in 1605, provides clear evidence of enclosures made in the common fields. Jeffrey Bushy reports that Sir Andrew Wood's workmen and labourers are 'dickinge an quicksetting in Langham field, and purposeth to in and inclose fyve hundret acars of arable land at the least besides that which he had taken in before tyme'. Celia Fiennes, on a long and observant journey on horseback at the close of the 17th century, wrote that 'Rutlandshire seems more woody and enclosed than some others'.

Leicestershire too abounds in evidence that enclosure and the change over to pastoralism was already extensive before the first of the Parliamentary acts in 1730. At Foston over half of the open fields were converted to pasture before Anthony Faunt, lord of the manor, proceeded to enclose in 1575. W.G. Hoskins, in his research into Leicestershire farming in the 16th century, has suggested that the early extension of pastures among the strips of the open arable fields was not accompanied 'by hedging and separating pieces of ground from the whole, but by leaving more and more strips in the open fields under ley for longer and longer periods'. The same move towards an increase in pasture that was to lead to enclosure and a radical reorganisation of farm holdings may be observed at Cossington, a large village that overlooks the flood-threatened triangle of lowland at the confluence of the Wreake and Soar. On the higher ground to east and south-east of the village, 600 acres of arable strips were spread across three great open fields. Contemporary documents of land holdings (terriers) show that farms of only moderate size were composed of numerous, scattered plots. For instance, Mistress Hulcock's 23 acres of arable were divided among 57 scattered strips. The full enclosure of Cossington did not take place until 1663, a time when much of the Leicestershire countryside was becoming laced with hedgerows. The final extinction of the common fields was achieved by agreement among the freeholders, which required no Act of Parliament. A majority of them appointed five commissioners whose task was to apportion land and to employ surveyors to carry out the work. 'The quantity, quality and convenience of every man's land' was considered in the making of the new compact farms that replaced the patchwork of scattered strips. It was arranged that the freehold cottagers – those with the right to graze a handful of livestock on the Wolds outside the rim of the arable fields – should receive land in compensation. The final enclosure of Cossington represents the end of a change to enclosed farming and pastoralism that had been going on there for at least half a century.

All over Leicestershire and Rutland local evidence suggests that enclosure was a long process of agricultural change that spanned the centuries between the later Middle Ages and the early years of Victoria's reign. It is the local expression of economic and social changes on a national scale – the rising demand for wool and meat, the increase of business in the land market towards the close of the 16th century, and the rise of the squirearchy and yeoman farmers. The trend towards pastoralism and the associated enclosure of the open fields was strong in Leicestershire because of the quality of its heavy clay soils and the accessibility of this part of the Midlands to the growing market for meat in London.

In the course of the 18th century the fattening of cattle that had journeyed on the hoof along the drove roads from the mountain pastures of Scotland and Wales became an ever increasing occupation of the county's graziers. Daniel Defoe on his tour through England and Wales in the early years of the 18th century noted the transformation that was taking place in Leicestershire's farming. 'The whole county seems to be taken up in country business, particularly in breeding and feeding cattle.' And again Leicestershire is 'a vast magazine of wool for the rest of the nation . . . in some places the graziers are so rich, that they grow gentlemen; tis not an uncommon thing for graziers here to rent farms from five hundred pounds to two thousand pounds a year rent'. Defoe was expressing his views of life and farming in Leicestershire a few years before the first of the county's parliamentary enclosure acts. The emergence of the rich yeomen, specialists in pastoral farming, is evident long before Defoe took his personal view of the county. We meet them in the *Inquisitions post mortem* of the late 16th century, wills of this rising class of farmers that could not yet call themselves gentlemen. Richard Bradgate died in 1572, the owner of 1,000 acres, most of which had been bought in land deals in the 1560s. In 1570, for instance, he purchased the manor of Bruntingthorpe of more than 500 acres from the Viscount Hereford. Richard Bradgate's *Inquisition post mortem* shows that livestock formed a greater part of his property. He owned 1,340 sheep and 82 head of cattle and horses. Much of his wealth was belonging to the deserted site of Knaptoft where the will tells us that 1,040 sheep, 40 oxen, 20 steers and kine, and nine horses grazed in Knaptoft pasture. Centuries later a 340-acre field at Knaptoft was known as Bradgate Field. Bradgate's estate in 1572 was worth £716 8s. 4d. He was far wealthier than many of those who called themselves gentlemen.

The rising yeoman farmers of the Tudor decades have left their mark on the Leicestershire landscape not only as pioneers of the enclosure movement but also in the buildings of the countryside. The history of Thomas Bent of Cosby and his son, John Bent, illustrates the investment of newly accumulated capital in fresh buildings. Within the space of eight years Thomas Bent bought the manor of Cosby and 660 acres of land as well as a number of houses and cottages. In the 1560s his son John spent money in building 'a mansion house' at Littlethorpe. His timber-framed house of close-set vertical posts still stands in the main street of Littlethorpe, a street whose name, Station Road, commemorates a Victorian revolution in technology that must have lain beyond the wildest imaginings of those up-and-coming Tudor yeomen. Only here and there has the great wave of rebuilding that accompanied the rising

Yeoman's house

prosperity of the yeoman survived for the enjoyment of 20th-century inhabitants. For instance, the Latymer House at Thurcaston, with a date on one of its beams of 1568, is a material sign of the wealth of an emerging rural middle class.

Latymer House, Thurcaston

Enclosure in the Leicestershire and Rutland countryside was far advanced a century before the first acts of parliament began a consistent record of these radical changes. It is estimated that by 1640, 25 per cent of the county of Leicestershire was enclosed; in other words, the enclosure movement had reached one in every three villages. In east Leicestershire village after village was completely enclosed by the time of the Civil War. As Dr. Joan Thirsk has written, 'in areas like this, where inclosure had achieved its greatest triumphs, the cause of open-field farming seemed in 1640 to be long since lost'.

It may seem surprising that local records contain so few references to opposition to enclosures that threatened the village peasantry with ruin. But, for example, the agreement to enclose the open fields of Cossington made provision for the various members of the community. A century earlier opposition to enclosure appeared in 1549 and 1553 with the ripping out of hedges and the filling in of ditches at places to which the record attaches no names. Ten men acknowledged 'their faulte committed of late in plucking upp of a hedge' and they were ordered 'to make upp the saide hedge agayne at thier costes and charges'. This was a minor local incident. The most determined act of opposition to enclosure happened at Cotesbach, on the southern fringe of Leicestershire, in 1607. This was at a time when enclosure was proceeding apace, when as much land had been enclosed in Leicestershire between 1600 and 1607 as had been in the previous half century. A new landlord at Cotesbach, John Quarles, had attempted enclosure ever since 1602. In 1607 opposition came to a head when 'men, women and children to the number of full five thousand' gathered there 'to level and lay open enclosures'.

The advantages and disadvantages of enclosures gave rise to much argument. Both sides of that argument were expressed in writings by clerics from parishes in south-west Leicestershire. In 1653, John Moore, minister of Knaptoft, published a pamphlet with the title of 'The crying Sin of England of not caring for the Poor'. It spoke for the peasantry who were cast into poverty by the extinction of the common lands. In the following year the rector of Catthorpe attempted to show that destitution and rural depopulation were not the inevitable result of enclosures. He compiled a list of villages that had been enclosed in the previous half century without a loss of population and 'without decay of tillage'. The debate continued through the era of parliamentary acts and enclosure awards. An anonymous pamphlet, published in 1778, tried to quantify the effects of the enclosure of the open fields upon village populations. The writer calculated that 1,000 acres of arable land in intermixed strips engaged 20 families; after enclosure the same area would support only five families. Later still, when the Leicestershire

73

and Rutland countryside was completely enclosed save for a handful of villages, parliamentary committees and royal commissions on agriculture had no conclusive evidence to show a dramatic upheaval of village populations at the time of enclosure. The vagabondage that seems to have accompanied the medieval desertions was not part of the reshaping of the countryside in the 18th century. Nevertheless, village histories of the early 19th century show that those who gained only a few acres at the time of enclosure gradually disappeared from the local scene. Years of unprofitable farming after the end of the Napoleonic Wars coupled with the attractions of growing industrial towns encouraged them to sell out to stronger neighbours. When Great Easton was enclosed in 1804 the smallest holdings of 10 acres and less numbered twenty-five. In the early 1820s, 11 of these small proprietors disappeared; their holdings were swallowed up into larger farms. Likewise, W.G. Hoskins has shown in his microscopic study of Leicestershire's rural history, *The Midland Peasant*, that towards the end of the 18th century the numbers of small landowners at Wigston Magna declined rapidly. Between 1781 and 1831 the number of small landowners who paid less than £2 in land tax fell from 33 to 22 landowners. Over the same time, the total number of proprietors at Wigston Magna fell from 94 to 64 landowners. Here, at this village within sight of the growing town of Leicester, we find the market in land stimulated by the demands of townspeople.

Windmill, Kibworth Harcourt

74

XII Roads and Canals

The web of roads, tracks and footpaths that covers Leicestershire and Rutland is as old as the presence of man himself in the East Midlands and it has evolved into its present pattern in response to economic needs and changing technology. The M1 motorway is only the most recent event in the history of the county's communications. That trade existed among Britain's prehistoric communities is undoubted, but the recognition and dating of prehistoric tracks is no easy task. Even the made roads of the Romans may be obscured by the works of later centuries and their very course is often a matter of conjecture after the quarrying of their gravel and stone foundations.

A post-enclosure road

The Jurassic Way was possibly a major line of communication across prehistoric England. Across south-east Leicestershire the course of this trail is marked by lanes that straddle the high ground between Kibworth and Tilton, but proof of their antiquity rests only on the fact that for some half-dozen miles the roads coincide with parish boundaries – a hint that here was a recognisable feature on the ground when those parishes were sketched out in late Saxon times. There is greater certainty about the early existence of a trackway across the eastern border of the county between the Trent and the Welland. The Sewstern Way is believed to date back to the Bronze Age. Its junction with Ermine Street, a mile to the south of Stretton in Rutland, suggests that it formed part of the road system of Roman Britain. The earliest documentary reference to the Sewstern Lane is in the 13th century, when the road was known as Shire Street. For several miles across this windy limestone upland to the north of Buckminster this disused trackway forms the boundary between the counties of Leicestershire and Lincolnshire. Before the coming of the railways it was regularly used by travellers between Nottingham and the Fens. Of late the building of a runway at Cottesmore's military airfield has broken this line of communication across Rutland that may have existed for almost 4,000 years.

Other roads whose existence in pre-Roman times may be accepted with some confidence include the lane that climbs eastward from Barrow upon Soar to follow a fairly direct line to the Sewstern Lane by Six Hills and the crest of the escarpment above the Vale of Belvoir. This too may form part of a Bronze Age network, and for three-quarters of its length, over a distance of 14 miles, the road acts as a boundary between parishes. Recent research has shown that Leicestershire and Rutland were more closely settled in prehistoric times than was previously

75

believed. Now it seems likely that many of the lanes are much older than was once thought, such as, for instance, the ridge-roads that reach from the Soar valley on the low ground about Leicester towards the upland plateau at Tilton. And the same speculation may apply in Rutland to the lane that follows the ridge between the Gwash and Chater through the site of the deserted village of Martinsthorpe.

*The
Loughborough
Navigation*

The legacy of Roman road-making has left a framework of communications to set the bounds for later development. Ermine Street strides across eastern Rutland close to the border with Lincolnshire. When Leicestershire was defined as a county, early in the 10th century, the line of Watling Street marked its western limit between the rivers Avon and Anker. Across the county from north-east to south-west runs the Fosse Way, part of a major line of communication that joined the Roman towns of Lincoln and Exeter. The Fosse Way is mentioned in a late Saxon charter of 956, but it seems highly likely that the route was part of the communications of prehistoric Britain for 2,000 years before the Roman conquest. The Romans came to define an ancient route with their radical methods of road construction and a system of organised posting stations placed at regular intervals.

Our knowledge of the network of Roman roads is probably far from complete. Over the past 2,000 years parts of the Roman system have been completely obliterated. The Gartree Road that branches south-eastward from the Fosse Way at Leicester formed part of a through route to Colchester. It was still an important approach to Leicester in the 16th century when the great topographer, Leland, came that way in Henry VIII's reign. Before the end of the 18th century the Gartree Road ceased to exist as a through route. For much of its length in the Welland valley the road was ploughed to its foundations. Elsewhere in the county fragments of road of Roman origin speak of a system the fullness of which remains to be revealed. For instance, a five-mile-long straight road from Watling Street by Fenny Drayton is undoubtedly of Roman origin, but its eastward course through Kirkby Malory and Peckleton towards Leicester, although known in part, still needs detailed location.

The development of the counties' roads between the Romans and the making of the first turnpike in 1726 is a most obscure topic. It is possible to speculate upon the opening up of fresh lines of communication but absolute proof is not to be found. For instance, the development of the road between Leicester and Loughborough along the Soar valley has been attributed to the passage of armies between Derby and Leicester – two of the garrisoned 'boroughs' in the Scandinavian occupation of the East Midlands at the close of the ninth century. The administration of the scattered manors of the Earl of Leicester in the 12th century may have led to the improvement of communications. It has been suggested that the present A50 to the west of Leicester began as a 'feudal road' from the town on the banks of the Soar to the earl's castle at Groby. Likewise there has been much speculation about the evolution of the two roads southwards from Leicester to London – one by Welford and

Northampton, the other through Market Harborough. The Welford road seems to have provided the earliest and most important route to London. Speed's map of 1610 describes it as 'the London waye', and it is believed to have been the primary road into Leicester long before the Norman Conquest. If there is anything in the contention that the line of the present A6 between Kibworth and Market Harborough was opened up only in the 12th century with the foundation of Market Harborough, then the Welford Road was for a long time the only route to the south.

The chief conclusion that can be drawn about the evolution of Leicestershire's road system is that the present network of communications had been substantially laid down before the Norman Conquest. Domesday Book's clear evidence that almost every village and hamlet was in being by the 11th century means that there must have been recognised tracks between these places. The contribution of the medieval centuries must have rested in the improvement of communications rather than the pioneering of fresh routes. Above all it is the securing of river-crossings by the construction of stone bridges and causeways that is attributable to these times. In Leicestershire alone a dozen bridges were built in the half century between 1272 and 1327. Five of these, at Kegworth, Zouch Bridge, Cotes, Cossington and Belgrave were concerned with the crossing of the county's most serious obstacle – the Soar below Leicester.

The 18th century saw the growth of long-distance traffic with time-tabled stage coaches. The necessary improvement of road surfaces and gradients brought the turnpike trusts into existence. Leicestershire's first turnpike was created by an Act of Parliament of 1726 that provided for the repairing of the 'principal road from London' through the county. This was the present A6 through Harborough, Leicester and Loughborough. The turnpike trust was empowered to make a gravel track 14 feet wide, of which every yard was to be made with five loads of road metal. By the 1760s the turnpike system had been extended to most of the main roads out of Leicester. The century of the turnpikes, before the railways put an end to all long-distance road traffic, saw many modifications and improvements in the old established road pattern. Many bridges were built or replaced. The first task of the Hinckley Turnpike Trust in 1754 was the building of bridges to replace the fords below Earl Shilton. The quarter century after the end of the Napoleonic War in 1815, and before the coming of the railways, is the classic period of road improvements. By now the great civil engineers whose skills had been acquired in the designing of canals applied their techniques to the improvement of roads. In 1810 a new section of the present A6 was built at Kibworth Harcourt to avoid the narrow twisting lane through the village. Further south, on the outskirts of Market Harborough, three quarters of a mile of new roads were constructed into the face of the prominent escarpment of Gallow Hill. *White's Directory* of 1846 shows that Leicestershire had 286 miles of turnpikes, but already their age of prosperity was over. The coming of the railways and the abandonment of the stage coaches between Manchester and London meant that the

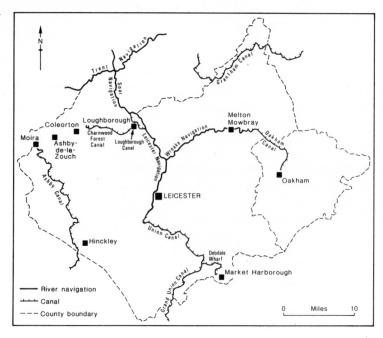

12. **Rivers and Canals.**

Harborough road lost one-third of its tolls. By the 1870s all the county's turnpike trusts had been wound up.

Although Leicestershire and Rutland lie in the heart of England far removed from coastal ports, they have not been excluded from the benefits given by water transport to the movement of heavy, bulky goods. The river Soar provided a natural line of transport that required improvement in places before barges could penetrate to Loughborough and Leicester. As early as 1634 Thomas Skipwith had obtained a grant of letters patent to make the Soar navigable from its outfall into the Trent as far as Leicester. But the times were not favourable to a project that would have extended the market for Derbyshire's coal into the East Midlands. Work on the improvement of the river navigation had to be abandoned for lack of money after five miles had been completed. The opening up of Leicestershire to water transport began only in the latter half of the 18th century. By 1778 Loughborough had become an inland port, joined to the Soar by the county's first canal, an artificial waterway of one-and-a-half miles in length. The Soar Navigation of these years was the work of Derbyshire coal owners and Loughborough businessmen, the same group that built the Erewash Canal to carry coal from the pits to the navigable Trent. Loughborough was transformed in the 1780s. Coal sold at less than two-thirds of its former price. A barge-building industry appeared and new houses and warehouses sprang up beside the wharves in the northern quarter of the town.

Foxton Locks on the Grand Union Canal

78

The improvement of the Soar to Leicester was proposed in 1779. Twelve years went by before the necessary Bill for the Leicester Navigation passed through parliament. Opposition to the improvement of the river had come from different directions. Owners of estates and mills on the banks of the river and the Soar Navigation with its profitable monopoly of the traffic to Loughborough did not like the idea, but the most virulent opposition came from the coal-owners of the West Leicestershire mines whose expensive fuel reached the Leicester market by cart and pack-horse along the Desford Coal Road. In 1791 the parliamentary bills for water transport were to open up much of the county. As well as access to Leicester by the main trunk of the Soar, the Wreake and Eye Navigation, sponsored by the Earl of Harborough, opened up the possibility of canal transport into Rutland. The interests of the Leicestershire coalfield were satisfied in the same year by the promise of a canal across the northern fringe of Charnwood Forest to the Soar at Loughborough that would allow their product to compete with the coal from the Erewash valley. Leicestershire was seized by canal mania in the 1790s.

At the end of February 1794 the Soar became navigable to Leicester. The effect on the borough in succeeding years, apart from a lowering in the cost of such heavy commodities as coal, bricks and lime, was a rapid growth in the north-eastern quarter of the town on both sides of Belgrave Gate. The hedge-lines of the earlier enclosed East Field of Leicester were to be replaced by the built-up streets of this first suburb of the industrial revolution. By the time of the completion of the Leicester Navigation some far-seeing minds already realised the position of Leicester and its river in a scheme of water communications that would join the Thames to the Trent, so providing a canal network linking London, Liverpool and Hull. Plans were already afoot in 1792 for the making of a canal to Market Harborough that would link up with the Leicester Navigation and an extension southwards to Northampton was proposed. In September 1792 the *Leicester Journal* contemplated the prospect of the county at the heart of a national network of water transport in which the borough would 'receive upon its quays the vessels from Thames and Trent — an inexhaustible source of commercial wealth'.

The extension of the canal southwards across the hills of the Leicestershire-Northamptonshire border was a long time in the making. By 1797 the works stopped short of Market Harborough at Debdale Wharf. The opposition of landowners had forced the expensive and physically unnecessary construction of the Saddington Tunnel and the war with France, started in 1793, introduced a long period of inflation that increased the financial risks of such major capital works. The short section to Market Harborough was not completed until 1809 and it was not until 1814, after the directors of the Grand Junction Company had combined with Leicester interests to form the Grand Union Canal Company, that the line of canals and river navigation was achieved from the Thames to the Humber.

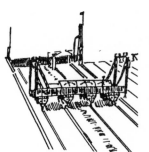

The inclined plane, Grand Union Canal, Foxton; opened in 1900, closed 1910

The canal mania of the early 1790s produced several schemes, some so wild and impracticable that they never came into being and others destined for financial failure. The Oakham Canal, an extension of the Wreake Navigation, received an Act of Parliament in 1793 and construction began in the following year. It was opened in June 1802 with wharves at Saxby, Stapleford, Market Overton, Cottesmore and Oakham. Deeply rural Rutland lacked the resources for industrial growth that were present in Leicester and the west of the county. Its countryside also lacked adequate supplies of water for the Oakham Canal and the frequent droughts of late spring and early summer hindered its traffic. Although the Oakham Canal was opened in 1802 its shareholders only began to receive regular dividend payments in 1827. The Leicestershire coalfield was tapped by the Ashby de la Zouch Canal whose bill, passed in 1794, heralded a decade of construction. Financial success was not part of its history. Opened in 1804, no dividend was paid until 1828 by which time, in a period of high inflation, the canal's original £100 shares had fallen to a value of £10. Four years later, when the Ashby de la Zouch Canal was beginning to show some return to its shareholders, the Leicester and Swannington Railway opened. A new age of transport was to spell the end of the canals.

Not all of Leicestershire's canals failed to express the hopes of their promoters. The Loughborough Navigation, built before the rising costs of the Revolutionary Wars, has been described as 'phenomenally prosperous'. Its canalisation of the Soar involved no exorbitant financial outlay and it answered the greatest commercial need of this part of the East Midlands. In 1804 the Loughborough Navigation's shares earned a 96 per cent dividend, and in 1824 the original £100 shares stood at £4,600. It was the very success of the traffic on the Soar that pushed the canal network into Leicestershire's unprofitable rural hinterland.

Today the influence of the brief canal era is imprinted on the county's landscape. The bed of the ill-fated Charnwood Forest canal may still be traced, in part, on the northern fringe of the Forest. Built to satisfy the demands of the Leicestershire coal owners at the time of the making navigable of the Soar above Loughborough, the canal was severely damaged within three years of its completion when spring thaws and floods after a severe frost burst the embankment of its feeder reservoir. But the most impressive relic of the age of water transport is the staircase of 10 locks at Foxton, built in 1812 as part of the Grand Union's link across the Northamptonshire upland to the Grand Junction at Long Buckby. An even more curious object of industrial archaeology is the inclined plane, beside the tier of Foxton locks, opened in 1900. By means of a steam-driven winch two narrow boats could be exchanged between the two levels of the canal in 12 minutes. The passage through the locks took 70 minutes. But such ingenious palliatives could not rescue the great volume of canal traffic that had long been diverted to the railways. By 1910 the Foxton Incline fell out of use and what traffic remained reverted to the locks. Today Foxton is a pleasure resort and the incline has been refurbished as a unique example of our industrial history.

32. Castle Donington — one of the several defunct market villages whose domestic architecture speaks of vanished trade and industry.

33. Victorian terrace, on the Danet's Hall estate, from the time of Leicester's most rapid period of growth in the latter part of the 19th century.

34. 'The Firs', Stoneygate, Leicester. A fine Regency house that announced the beginning of a wealthy residential suburb along the London Road on an airy ridge to the south-east of the medieval borough. The house is now the centre of 'The Islamic Foundation'.

35. Mount St Bernard in Charnwood Forest is the first Catholic abbey founded in England since the Reformation. Its inspiration came from Ambrose Lisle March Phillips de Lisle whose estate at Garendon had taken the site of a former Cistercian monastery. Augustus Pugin was the architect for this Cistercian house of Mount St Bernard where building began in 1849.

36. West Langton Hall. Unlike Northamptonshire, Leicestershire is lacking the greatest and grandest of country houses, but there are many small-scale residences of the county's gentry built out of the profits of sheep pastures and cattle-fattening meadows. West Langton Hall belongs to the heyday of the English country house in the Georgian decades.

37. Staunton Harold, a grand Palladian house, started in the 1760s around an early 17th-century building, in warm red brick and creamy limestone.

38. Foxton Locks on the Grand Union Canal: two staircases of five locks were completed in 1812 shortly before the link with the Grand Junction Canal opened a water route from Leicester to London.

39. The Grand Union Canal at Debdale Wharf. From 1797 until 1814 this was the terminus of the canal that aimed to provide a water route from Leicester to London. Work ceased because of lack of capital as well as the expensive obstacle of the high ground that had to be breached to link up with the Grand Junction Canal. Only in 1814 did the great inland water route from the Thames to the Trent and Humber become a reality.

XIII The Leicestershire Coalfield

The north-western fringe of Leicestershire, the territory of one of Britain's smallest coalfields, has always stood aloof from the rest of the county. The separateness of the coalfield is exaggerated by the barrier of hills that Charnwood Forest places between it and the heart of Leicestershire in the Soar valley. Even more, the distinctiveness of the north-west rests in the mining of coal, an occupation that dates back in the records to the early years of the 13th century. Its present landscape reflects the dominant occupation of the region. Shapeless brick-built villages, a handful of surviving collieries, one of England's earliest railways and the scars of centuries of digging for coal are all proof of this.

The coalfield, covering some 60 square miles, forms an extension across a dividing county boundary of the South Derbyshire coalfield. The seams of coal and their associated beds of sandstone, shales and clays are folded into two basins which are separated from each other by an upfold, the Ashby anticline, whose crest trends in a generally north-west to south-east direction passing through Ashby de la Zouch and Packington. The vertical section of the coal-bearing rocks, almost 1000 feet thick, divides into the Upper Coal Measures, known as the Productive Series, and the Lower Coal Measures with scarcely any workable coal seams, which is called the Unproductive Series. The coal-bearing rocks of the Upper Productive Measures were stripped by erosion from the exposed Asbhy anticline some 250 million years ago before the deposition of the thick red mudstones of Triassic age that hide the southern part of the coalfield today. Because of the absence of economically productive coal seams throughout a zone of country that coincides with the Ashby anticline, the history of the Leicestershire coalfield has been split into two districts. The eastern coalfield lies between the Ashby anticline and the abrupt western flank of Charnwood Forest. The western sector of the coalfield reaches southwards from the Derbyshire border as far as Measham. In both parts of the coalfield there are some 20 workable coal seams and in its busiest times the annual output has reached more than 3,000,000 tons.

The earliest evidence of mining in Leicestershire dates back to the beginning of the 13th century. A charter of 1204 confirms the gift of land 'worth two shillings per annum in Swannington where cole is found'. Three other documents before the end of the 13th century tell of coal mining. In 1270, Garendon Abbey was given 'the whole wood at Worthington with the whole soil to the same adjacent, with the common

81

of pasture, coalmines, and all other appurtenances'. A record from 1293 survives of an annual rent of four cartloads of coal arising from land at Donington-le-Heath.

If the surviving documents are held to tell the whole of the early history of coal mining in Leicestershire, then it would seem that the eastern part of the coalfield (centred on Swannington) has a longer history of exploitation than that of the coal seams outcropping to west of the Ashby anticline. The earliest reference to the west occurs in a rental of Leicester Abbey that tells us that the monks possessed a coal mine at Oakthorpe in 1477. But history derived solely from documents can never be complete either because of loss or incomplete records in the first place. There is no evidence that the Romans mined coal in Leicestershire, although the outcrop of seams at the surface in the exposed part of the coalfield to the north of Whitwick could have presented few obstacles. Yet the evidence, published by Professor Sir Ian Richmond, that coal from Nottinghamshire was burned at Roman sites in Lincolnshire suggests that Leicestershire might also have had a part to play in this exploitation of the East Midland's coal deposits 1,000 years before the beginning of the documentary records. In his *History of the Moira Collieries*, published in 1919, Beaumont maintained that coal mining there began in prehistoric times. It was based on the evidence of a find of stone hammers, flints and solid wooden discs whose age is unknown and whose connection with coal mining is unproven. But of mining in the Middle Ages there is no doubt. Its scale must have been small, from open pits that tapped the seams nearest the surface. Of the organisation of the industry the documents tell us that at Swannington any freeman could dig coal on the common land of the township, while at Worthington and Staunton Harold exploitation was in the hands of the lord of the manor. By the end of the 15th century the importance of mining in north-west Leicestershire is suggested in a document of 1498 that describes two of the inhabitants of Coleorton as *collyers*. Mining seems to have been recognised as a profession.

Moira furnace

More detailed evidence about the working of the pits at Coleorton during Elizabeth I's reign has survived. Three manuscripts relate to the pits there in the 1570s. The *Collpit Book* and the *Synkinge Book* provide details of mining operations in the last two months of 1572. The former shows that miners worked in gangs of up to 20 men and that they were paid collectively at the end of the week. The *Synkinge Book*, as its name implies, preserves details of the extension of the mine at Coleorton. Men engaged in driving new headings there were paid sixpence per day and their employer provided tools and candles and also paid for the sharpening of the tools. The third manuscript source, a statement of account, dates from November 1577. It shows the output of coal over the previous 12 months. Seven thousand rooks were extracted. The problem for the modern economic historian is to know how much is actually meant by a *rook*. It seems to have been a stack of coal of fixed dimensions that contained, it is estimated, between one and two tons.

82

The pits at Coleorton were worked by Sir Francis Willoughby who leased the coal rights in this part of the exposed coalfield from Nicholas Beaumont, lord of the manor of Coleorton. Sir Francis Willoughby was a pioneer among landowners of the exploitation of the mineral wealth beneath his properties. Towards the end of the 16th century he owned mines in Nottinghamshire, Derbyshire and Warwickshire as well as in Leicestershire. On his estate at Wollaton, on the outskirts of Nottingham, stands the visual realisation of his economic activities – Wollaton Hall, one of the most important Elizabethan houses in England.

By the end of the 16th century, coal mining was an important occupation in west Leicestershire. It has been estimated that in the 1570s Coleorton Colliery alone was capable of an output of 10,000 tons in a year. The chief market seems to have been in the town of Leicester whose borough records show that the authorities laid in stocks of coal for the poor. Coal brought from Coleorton was carried by pack horse down to the crossing of the Soar by Braunstone Lane – formerly known as Coal Pit Lane. Even so the working of the easily accessible seams of the exposed coalfield made little impact on the landscape apart from the hollows and hillocks on ground pock-marked with the bell-pit method of extraction. Mining too was a seasonal occupation, frequently interrupted for weeks on end in late winter when flooding interfered with working. By the end of the 18th century notable changes had overtaken the techniques and organisation of the industry. John Prior's map of Leicestershire, published in 1779, shows 37 pits scattered across the outcrops of the exposed coalfield. There are seven in the western part of the coalfield between Oakthorpe and Measham and as many as 20 in the vicinity of Coleorton and Swannington.

Descriptions in Nichols' *The History and Antiquities of the County of Leicester* that appeared in four volumes between 1795 and 1811 show the scale of mining operations during the 18th century. Nichols records the sinking of two pits on Swannington Common by Gabriel Holland in 1760 to reach the deeper riches of the Stone Smut Seam and the Nether Coal. An elliptical-shaped shaft, brick-lined, was sunk and above it was a gin wheel with pulleys whose power was supplied by horses. Stables with accommodation for 40 horses were also built on the site of Gabriel Holland's coal mine. The scale of mining in 18th-century Swannington is also revealed by a lawsuit of 1794 that concerned the Silver Hill workings of John Wilkins. He employed 300 men and a 'sough', a tunnel driven into the mine for the purpose of drainage, had cost several hundred pounds.

The chief obstacle to the expansion of the Leicestershire coalfield up to the close of the 18th century was the lack of cheap transport. An extension of its market beyond the immediate neighbourhood and the borough depended upon the provision of water transport that would allow the coal owners to compete with their closest rivals in Nottinghamshire who were blessed with the natural waterway of the Trent and, by the turn of the century, with a growing canal network. The first notable improvement for the Leicestershire coalfield was the completion of the Charnwood Forest Canal in 1794. The Ashby Canal opened up the western half of the coalfield in the first decade of the 19th century. The Earl of Moira, the chief promoter of the canal, began the sinking of Double Pits on Ashby Woulds in 1804. Here a steam engine was used for the haulage of coal, the first use of steam power for winding in Leicestershire. Two years later the sinking of the Furnace Pits began, and by 1812 work was begun on the Main Coal at a depth of more than 600 feet. In 1813 Lord Moira extended his investment in the western part of the coalfield with the opening of the Bath Pits close to the canal. The basin of the Ashby Canal on the Woulds became the focus of a network of tramways that reached out to collieries at Heather, Norman-ton-le-Heath, Lount and Staunton Harold. Parts of this tramway system, using horse traction, were to be absorbed in the railway network that proved to be the most important factor in the evolution of the coalfield after 1832.

The 19th century saw the full development of the Leicestershire coalfield. The deepest seams were opened up, new pits extended the area of mining into the 'hidden coalfield' where the Coal Measures lie buried beneath a thick cover of the red rocks of the Trias, and in the most favourable years the highest outputs, reaching 3,500,000 tons, were achieved. The Leicestershire and Swannington Railway that wound through the pleasant countryside of the hidden coalfield to link up with the old tramway system between the Ashby Canal and Breedon largely determined the location of the new mines later in the 19th century, although the architects of the railway were not unmindful of the mining enterprise that was already stirring in the concealed coalfield in the 1820s. The first to breach the cover of Triassic rocks was a farmer at Ibstock who sank a 200-foot shaft in 1825. A year later Viscount Maynard established a large colliery on his manor at Bagworth. The Whitwick Colliery opened at Long Lane in 1824 to exploit a coal seam at a depth of 350 feet. This colliery and the railways which followed led to the creation of Coalville, now the county's third largest town outside Leicester. Close by houses were built to house the miners on Whitwick's Waste, but even when the Leicester and Swannington Railway was opened in 1833 there was found to be no need for a station at Long Lane to serve the new settlement. After the opening of the Whitwick Colliery a second focus of settlement appeared with the establishment of a mine at Snibston, a mile to the west, in 1831. Here the new enterprise was directed by George Stephenson who with the aid of capital from merchants in Liverpool was able to foresee the economic advantages that the Leicester and Swannington Railway was about to confer. Stephenson and his partners built the village of Snibston, a typical straggly mining settlement alongside the turnpike from Leicester to Ashby de la Zouch. By 1846 the four shafts of Snibston Colliery were drawing coal from depths of 700 feet and the new mining community that had come into being between the two collieries housed a population of 1,200 people.

The earliest appearance of its name in the documents is the record of 'Whitwick-Coalville' in the County Rate Return. By 1847 the opening of a railway station at Coalville confirmed the existence of this new town, born out of the expansion of Leicestershire's coal mining.

In the last quarter of the 19th century the coalfield reached maturity. The last mine of the hidden coalfield was sunk at Desford in 1900. The shaft passed through more than 300 feet of red marls and sandstones before it touched the first seam of coal. Below that another 500 feet of rock, containing 20 seams of coal, was penetrated. The busy decade of the 1870s began the shaping of the coalfield as it is today. For the first time, in 1874, the output of the Leicestershire mines reached more than 1,000,000 tons. In 1876 new pits were opened at Hugglescote, Ellistown and Nailstone, and in the following year the Whitwick Colliery reached a depth of 915 feet in a seam of high quality coal known as 'the Roaster'. This was the time of much building of red-brick miners' terraces along country roads in the southern part of the coalfield.

Growth came to an end after the opening of the Desford pit in 1900. The 20th century is a tale of fluctuating prosperity and decline in the Leicestershire coalfield. In the years of depression, between 1927 and 1933, the annual output of coal fell by almost 1,000,000 tons. Within the oldest part of the coalfield, on the exposed Coal Measures, a new colliery was opened up. This was at Lount, and was opened up in 1924, only to be closed after the Second World War in the severe rationalisation of the industry under the National Coal Board.

Leicestershire's small coalfield, however, has retained a place in British mining on account of its efficiency. At the beginning of this century its average output per man was well above that of the rest of the United Kingdom's coal industry. In the years between the First and Second Wars Leicestershire was well ahead in the investment in machinery for coal cutting and haulage. Now it is the limited resources of this coalfield after eight centuries of recorded exploitation that over-shadow the future, a future in which the recently discovered untapped wealth of coal beneath the Vale of Belvoir threatens to shift the focus of coal mining to the east of the county.

Colliery at Ellistown

85

XIV The Georgian Town

Social and economic changes in the life of a community find a reflection in the surrounding landscape. Leicestershire in the 18th century was deeply affected by the progress of enclosures and the growth of the hosiery industry that had taken root in market towns and villages before 1700. Important too in the shaping of Leicestershire during the 18th century was a notable increase in population, an increase that was to make its greatest impact in places that favoured the hosiery industry.

The history of Leicestershire's population, drawn from imprecise sources before the first national census in 1801, shows that a period of expansion through the 18th century had followed several decades of stagnation in the time of the Stuarts and the Commonwealth. The main source of information about the 18th-century population lies in the statistics of baptisms, burials and marriages contained in parish registers. They reveal a population that was on the increase after 1740 and whose growth was particularly accelerated at the close of the century. An estimate of Leicestershire's population, calculated from parish registers, produces a total of 80,000 in 1700 and of a little more than 98,000 in 1750. The first census in 1801 showed that the population had reached 130,000. Much of this increase contributed to the growth of the county town and the places where the seeds of the new industry had been sown. In Leicester we find that the *Register of Apprentices* records a constant flow of young men into the borough from the countryside for ten miles around. Over the century expansion was rapid in Loughborough and Hinckley. Returns made for the bishop of Lincoln in units of families showed that Loughborough had 530 families in 1705 and at the beginning of the 19th century there were 1,000 families, Anglicans, Catholics and Dissenters, in the town. Hinckley likewise had grown from about 300 families to almost one thousand. Growth over the same period of a century seems to have proceeded much more slowly in the small market towns of rural east Leicestershire where the impact of the hosiery industry was negligible. Melton Mowbray rose from about 300 to 358 families in the bishops' surveys. The 18th century saw some of the smaller market villages forced from stagnation into decline. The number of families in Billesdon fell from 150 to 127 between 1705 and 1801.

The most spectacular rise in population over the 18th century belongs to Leicester. In 1801, according to the census returns, the borough housed 16,953 people; at the beginning of the 18th century the total was only about 6,000 people. The rise in numbers was accompanied by

St Dionysius,
Market
Harborough

86

striking changes in the face of the town. Two much quoted observations of travellers in the 17th century record the decline into obscurity of a great medieval town. In Charles II's time, Thomas Baskerville was downright in his condemnation. He wrote, 'it is now an old stinking town, situated upon a dull river inhabited for the most part by tradesmen ... stinking puddles made me go spewing through all the streets, yet it hath formerly been a town of good remark'. That the face of the medieval borough was little changed by the end of the 17th century is confirmed by Celia Fiennes who found Leicester a place of 'old timber buildings except one or two of brick'. One hundred years later Leicester was in the midst of a phase of rebuilding that was to remove almost every visible trace of the Middle Ages from the urban scene.

The political history of Georgian Leicester comes to an end with the passing of the Municipal Corporation Reform Act in 1835, an act of parliament that extinguished the power of the Tory group which had dominated the life of the borough through the 18th century. In the closing years of the 'old corporation', Leicester had become a by-word for inefficiency and corruption. The census of 1831 shows that the town's population had grown to about 40,000 people. Here was a thriving, expanding industrial town with a population of hosiers, frame-owners, craftsmen and apprentices, fed by a stream of immigrants from the surrounding countryside; a strongly nonconformist community which lacked any say in the management of the borough. The 'old corporation' was too weak to control the growing hosiery industry and incapable of involving the new elements in the life of Leicester. Consequently its record through the 18th century showed a government that was 'more and more inclined to care only for the personal interests of its own exclusive membership'. Even so, Georgian Leicester has coloured the townscape of the 20th-century city. The focus of the inner city shifted through the decades of the 18th century from the western quarter around the crossing of High Street and High Cross Street to the east, outside the line of the wall where four roads – Churchgate, Belgravegate, Humberstone Gate and Gallowtree Gate – converged at the entrance to the inner town, the hundred acres within the wall that had marked the heart of an urban community in Roman, Saxon and medieval times. The principal inns of the 18th century lay in this quarter. Before the end of the 18th century improved communications through the growing network of turnpike roads and the timetabled journeys of stage coaches gave Leicester regular contact with distant towns and cities. By the 1760s the journey from Leicester to London could be made in one day. These regular contacts with the capital allowed some of the habits of London life to take root in this provincial market town. Towards the end of the 18th century a coffee house was established where the previous day's London papers, brought by the mail coach, could be read.

Several attractive pieces of the landscape of Georgian Leicester contribute to the make-up of the modern city. The most valuable part of this legacy is New Walk, a tree-lined promenade that was laid out in

Wyggeston House

1785 along the boundary of the South Field. This pedestrian precinct preserved a much older line of communication into the borough because it is believed that the Roman Gartree road, joining Colchester with the Midlands, followed the same direction to make its junction with the Fosse Way in Leicester. Building along New Walk began in the early years of the 19th century when small plots of land were sold to help meet the cost of the enclosure of the 600-acre South Field for which an Award had been granted in 1811. Today a leisurely stroll from the city's shopping street to the wide grassy space of Victoria Park along the traffic-free New Walk reveals the changing styles of 19th-century upper-class domestic architecture. Now it is largely a street of offices – accountants, solicitors and the regional bases of national companies – but central to this half-mile long promenade and to its building history is the Museum of 1836 with its over-powering columned portico.

Developments in the 18th century considerably changed the street plan in the core of the city. The main network of streets had been in existence from before the Norman Conquest and their presence is attested in the borough records from the end of the 12th century. The years after 1700 saw the first important additions to a medieval pattern of roads. New Street, connecting Peacock Lane and Friar Lane, was laid out in 1711. Between 1808 and 1809 Bishop Street and Belvoir Street were sketched out to the south of the line of the former medieval wall on the enclosed land of the former East Field. The enclosure of the South Field in 1811 was followed by the laying out of a mosaic of new streets on land acquired by the Corporation at the time of the enclosure. Here Hastings Street, King Street, Regent Road, Princess Road and Lancaster Road mark the development of a new middle-class suburb beyond the bounds of the old city.

The earliest signs of Leicester's development as an industrial town appear in the 18th century. In 1792, one of the first factories, built for the spinning of cotton, was opened in Northgate Street. But it was on the East Field, whose Enclosure Act of 1764 had provided land ripe for private development, that Leicester's chief industrial quarter evolved in the early years of the 19th century. In the parish of St Margaret's, between Humberstone Gate and the wharfs of the Leicester Navigation, the nucleus of the industrial city of the 19th century appeared. The first census of 1801 showed that St Margaret's parish numbered 6,000 people. By the end of the century the population figures approached 100,000 and the huge medieval parish had been carved up into 11 separate parishes serving the acres of densely packed terraced housing and Victorian factories.

Belgrave Hall built for Edmund Craddock about 1710; now in the care of Leicester Museums

Even villages beyond the immediate orbit of 18th-century Leicester were not untouched by the borough's demographic and economic upsurge. Belgrave became favoured as a residential suburb after Edward Craddock had completed the building of Belgrave Hall in 1713. A century later the village had been transformed into an outlier of industrial Leicester. The Leicester Navigation skirted the western fringe of the village in 1791; by 1800 it was noted that hosiery had taken the place of agriculture as the chief occupation of the inhabitants of Belgrave. Even so, Belgrave did not become a city-suburb until the massive Victorian expansion of Leicester had taken place. In the 1850s the Melton Road still ran through fields in Belgrave township and it was only in 1892, when the population of the village had reached 12,000, that Belgrave was absorbed into Leicester.

Ashby-de-la-Zouch – the Ivanhoe Baths of 1882

The rapid growth of Leicester and its population in the 18th century is mirrored, though to a lesser degree, in the market towns and villages of the county. Some places declined in importance over the century. Billesdon and Hallaton, for instance, housed smaller populations than they had 100 years earlier. Others grew but did so slowly. Melton Mowbray sheltered 351 families in 1801; in 1705 there had been 300 families. Market Harborough reveals a more active history in the 18th century. Its parish records show an increase in the number of families from 420 to 538 in 1801. But the greatest energy is displayed in the towns where the hosiery industry became firmly rooted. Loughborough doubled in size and the population of Hinckley trebled between 1700 and 1801.

By the 18th century Leicester, like many other towns in both Leicester-shire and Rutland, could boast its own Free Grammar School. Despite its name, this catered mainly for the children of the more prosperous, and the children of poor parents were generally provided for in charity schools attached to churches of different denominations. St Mary de Castro, for instance, supported a school from 1785. The 17th century had seen the foundation – or in some cases the re-foundation – of a number of schools, including for instance that at Osgathorpe, built in conjunction with an almshouse, or at Billesdon, where both George Villiers, the first duke of Buckingham and favourite of James I and Charles I, and George Fox the Quaker received their early education. Another school with interesting associations is that of Market Bosworth, founded early in the 16th century, where Samuel Johnson spent an unhappy period as a teacher in the 18th century. There were also many small village establishments resulting from the charity of well-to-do local gentry, like that at Thrussington, founded with funds left by Sir Thomas Hayne in the early 17th century for the education of 10 poor children of his native village.

None of Leicestershire's educational establishments of this date, how-ever, has become so well-known beyond its own locality as the Rutland schools of Oakham and Uppingham. The school at Oakham was origi-nally attached to the church, and the 16th-century vicarage is still part of the school premises, as is the building in the churchyard which was for 300 years the only classroom and is now the school's museum. Both schools were founded in 1584 by Archdeacon Robert Johnson. Up-pingham too was for many years no more than a single building in the churchyard. Both had to wait until the 19th century for their transformation into the large public schools of today.

Market Harborough originated as a new founded town in the parish of Great Bowden before the end of the 12th century. Professor Hoskins has proposed that its inception lay in the rising trade of the 12th century that felt the need for a settlement, a stopping place with markets and fairs, on the long road between Northampton and Leicester. The same factor, Market Harborough's passing traffic, seems to have been largely responsible for its growth and prosperity in the 18th century. By 1755 the long High Street, the market street, on the north bank of the Welland, found itself at the nexus of four turnpiked roads. By the 1760s Harborough's inns dispatched six coaches daily to London and their direct services stretched northwards to Derby and Nottingham. The establishment of additional fairs tells of Market Harborough's enlarged traffic in the late 18th century. Until 1750 the October fair, founded early in the 13th century, sufficed. Then a new fair, held at the end of April, was founded. In 1772 additional fairs, in January and July, were introduced. By 1800 three more fair days had come into being. John Nichols in his classic *History and Antiquities of Leicestershire*, written between 1795 and 1811, caught the character of Georgian Market Harborough in two words when he described it as a 'thoroughfare town'.

Of all the towns of Leicestershire, Market Harborough displays the Georgian years to the best advantage. The High Street that now bears the incessant traffic of the A6 is the result of major replanning in 1776. Before that date a tributary stream to the Welland flowed the whole length of the market street and there was a roadway on either side. This street presents an attractive array of Georgian building dating from the latter years of the 18th century. The three-storeyed red-brick town hall was built by the Earl of Harborough in 1788 to serve as a market hall and assembly rooms. In 1809 Harborough's importance was signalled by the opening of a branch from the Grand Union Canal. As in so many other English rural market towns, it was the coming of the railways and the abrupt cessation of the stage coach traffic that sent Market Harborough into a decline. Although Harborough became a junction of secondary importance in the East Midland railway system, this was insufficient to compensate for the loss of its road traffic. Now, in the latter half of the 20th century, Market Harborough's place in the English road network has been restored.

·Oakham market cross

In all the other market towns of Leicestershire and Rutland, there is visual evidence from the years about 1800. At Oakham, Lutterworth, Melton Mowbray and Uppingham street plans, inherited from earlier centuries, remained little changed by the developments of the Georgian years. The legacy of 18th-century changes consists of the replacement and rebuilding of existing houses in which timber, thatch and local stone give way to brick and, here and there, the erection of public buildings to serve new economic and social functions. At Lutterworth the bridge over the river Swift, at the south entrance to the town, was rebuilt in 1778 in response to the rising traffic of the stage coach years. A town hall followed in the 1830s as well as the growth of a late Georgian quarter at the west end of the town. Oakham was substantially rebuilt in the 18th century, so much so that Professor Hoskins, in an atmospheric guide to Rutland, compares the town unfavourably with Uppingham on account of its 'more unseemly red brick'. The most interesting of the small towns of this period in Leicestershire is undoubtedly Ashby de la Zouch. There is a familiar long wide market street where, over the years, fire and fashion changed an older medieval market village into the typical brick-faced Georgian town. As Pevsner comments, 'there are no buildings of note in the street'. Development close to the lower end of Market Street in the 1820s stamped Ashby de la Zouch with the character of Georgian England. The most successful of Leicestershire's spas came into existence here, based on piped water from a mineral spring at Moira Colliery. The Royal Hotel, terraced houses of the period and the former Ivanhoe Baths (the name playing upon Ashby's associations with Scott's romantic historical novel) all combined to form a tiny late Georgian quarter – a gem of its kind in the Leicestershire urban scene.

18th-century wrought iron inn sign –
The Three Swans, *Market Harborough*

XV Hosiery, Shoes, Machinery

Leicestershire's industrial revolution begins with the introduction of hand-worked knitting frames for the manufacture of stockings early in the 17th century. The stocking frame, the essential tool of the cottage-based hosiery industry, had been invented by William Lee of Calverton, Nottinghamshire, in 1589. For almost half a century, before the first stocking frame appeared in Leicestershire at Hinckley in 1640, hosiery making in the hands of William Lee and his brother James had been carried on in London, in Nottingham, and for some years on the continent at Paris. Hosiery making with the use of Lee's stocking frame took root in the East Midlands partly because of the Lee family's association with Nottingham but also because of the growing use of wool, and later cotton, in a market that had originally been confined to silk. As the product became cheaper so the market extended. The demand for labour in the growing hosiery trade stimulated the move from London where the rules of the Company of Framework Knitters limited the number of apprentices.

William Iliffe began the manufacture of hosiery at Hinckley, as far as can be known, about the year 1640. By the latter half of the 17th century the detailed lists of possessions in Leicestershire wills show that the industry was widely rooted in the countryside. The earliest will that makes mention of a stocking frame is the inventory of George Hogsonn of Dishley Mill, dated 4 February 1660. One hundred years later framework knitting was widely spread through the Leicestershire countryside; in the latter part of the 18th century it is evident in 118 of the county's villages and hamlets. The wills of the 18th century show that it was usually combined with farming. One Jenings Berrington of Hathern, a framework knitter who died in 1740, was the owner of land in the open fields as well as 'four cow pastures'. Leicester, the place that was to emerge as the capital and organising focus of the hosiery trades in the 19th century, preserves no evidence of stocking frames in the borough earlier than the 1670s.

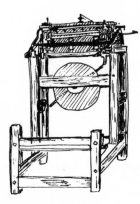

Stocking frame

By the end of the 18th century hosiery-making dominated the industries of Leicestershire. William White, in his *History, Gazetteer and Directory of Leicestershire*, states that nearly half of Leicester's population in 1801 depended on hosiery and that the rise of this industry through the 18th century lay behind the growth of the borough – its population trebled between 1700 and 1800. John Nichols too, researching his great county history at the end of the 18th century, estimated that 43 per cent of

92

Leicestershire's population was dependent upon 'one branch of trade', hosiery. In the 1660s it seems there were about 50 frames in the whole of Leicestershire. One hundred years later the number had risen to about 1,000 frames, but by 1812, towards the close of a long period of prosperity during the Revolutionary and Napoleonic Wars, there were more than 11,000 stocking frames employed in Leicester and the surrounding countryside. Towards the middle of the 19th century, before the eclipse of the widespread cottage industry by the steam-powered factories in Leicester, Hinckley and Loughborough, the number of knitting frames exceeded more than 20,000 in total. However, by the 1840s, many of these were idle. Felkin, in his history of the hosiery and lace industries published in 1867, estimated that one-third of the stocking frames in Leicester were already out of use in the 1840s.

Knitted hosiery was a name for many products – stockings, socks, shirts, gloves and cravats. Lace-making, pioneered by John Heathcoat of Loughborough, developed from the older industry. An accident of history was responsible for the early demise of lace-making in Leicestershire. After a wave of machine smashing in the Luddite riots of 1816 Heathcoat moved his lace manufactures from Loughborough to Tiverton in Devon.

Leicestershire's framework knitters enjoyed a long period of prosperity from the 1780s until the end of the Napoleonic Wars. The years of the French Wars made great demands on the industry. Labour was scarce and workers were attracted to the hosiery villages and Leicester from beyond the county's boundaries in Warwickshire and Northamptonshire. Deep economic depression followed the victory of Waterloo in 1815 and the ending of the war. Returning soldiers added to the surfeit of labour. The report of a parliamentary commission on the framework knitters, published in 1845 showed that between 1815 and 1819 the wages for a full week's work of 15 hours per day had fallen from 14s. to 7s. But this was only the beginning of the decline of the rural hosiery industry that continued for the greater part of the 19th century.

The development of machines that displaced the man-powered knitting frames makes a late appearance in the long story of decline. The first steam-powered hosiery factory had opened at Loughborough in 1839, but in the middle of the 19th century, power-driven machinery in the hosiery industry was still a novelty. The extinction of the rural framework knitter came only in the 1860s. In 1864 William Cotton patented a machine that opened the way to the concentration of the industry in steam-powered factories. By 1871 there were 74 factories in the county. During the last quarter of the 19th century the rural manufacture of hosiery on a domestic scale vanished. Several other factors, over more than half a century, contributed to the decline of the scattered, family-based industry. Not least among them were the whims of changing fashion. 'Fancy hosiery' was at its zenith in the years about 1800. The Leicester hosiers, merchants who provided yarn to the village knitters and frequently hired out their frames as well as marketing the finished products, complained that the long depression resulted from the loss of foreign trade. William Biggs, in 1845, declared that the American exports had been captured by 'German manufacturers in Saxony'.

The boot and shoe industry lies second in importance to hosiery in the industrial history of Leicestershire. At its peak, early in the 20th century, the boot and shoe factories found employment for 35,000 people and at the outbreak of the First World War there were 165 firms in the city and another 85 scattered through the villages. The geographical pattern of the industry in the 19th century closely resembles that of hosiery-making, a fact that is largely explained by the close connections with the older industry in the formative stage of boot and shoe manufacturing in the 1850s and '60s.

The shoemaker was part of the economic life of every community in the Middle Ages. Leicester's shoe making industry emerged from radical changes in marketing and methods of manufacture after the middle of the 19th century. White's *Directory of Leicestershire and Rutland*, published in 1846, lists 200 boot- and shoe-makers in the borough of Leicester. One of these, Thomas Crick, with premises in Highcross Street, is described as a wholesaler. Already Crick had distinguished himself in exploiting a wider market than that of his neighbourhood. In the next two decades he was outstanding among the first generation of industrialists in Leicester. In 1853 Thomas Crick patented a machine for the riveting of the soles of shoes to their uppers. About the year 1855 a machine that could sew leather was imported from the United States and in 1858 an even more important invention from America, Blake's sole-sewing machine, eased the way towards mass production and the transformation of boot- and shoe-making into a factory industry. The appearance of boot and shoe factories in Leicester by the early 1860s is clearly seen in the evidence that the *Royal Commission on the Employment of Children* published in its *Second Report* in 1864. One witness attested that 'the wholesale boot and shoe trade in Leicester may be said to have come into existence within the last five years'. Crick's factory employed 300 men and 420 women and children (some of whom were as young as twelve). At that time Crick's factory was the only one in the county in which steam power was applied to sewing machines.

Until the end of the century shoe manufacturers multipled in Leicester. By 1880 there were 198 different firms in the borough and by 1900 the number had risen to 225 firms. Work was found for 24,000 people. At the same time the boot and shoe industry spread into the countryside. In the 1850s and '60s a method of production, known as the 'basket-work system', arose in which the uppers were cut and closed in the factory while the 'making' of the shoe – the attachment of the soles to the uppers by wax-thread sewing – was completed in small workshops in the villages. An examination of the places where this new industry appeared shows that the manufacture of boots and shoes in the mid-19th century was putting down roots in the villages where the hosiery industry

94

was beginning to fail. Thomas Crick, for example, handed out work to the decaying framework knitting village of Earl Shilton. In Barwell, Sileby and Anstey, among other places, outworkers took over the attics and sheds that once housed the stocking frames. White's *Directory* of 1863 records one 'boot-and-shoe manufacturer' at Anstey; by 1870 there were three more. At the close of the century boot and shoe making, the whole process under the roof of one factory, was firmly established in the countryside around Leicester. In 1896 there were 17 'wholesale and export boot and shoe manufacturers' in Anstey. And the same directory records 15 at Hinckley, 12 at Earl Shilton, 11 at Barwell and four in Shepshed. By that time the 'basket-work system' had died out.

Several causes explain the extinction of the old system – not least the increasing complexity of machinery, the widespread use of the gas engine as a source of power, and also the influence of The National Union of Boot and Shoe Operatives on the growth of th industry. The Union, formed in 1874, had become the fourth largest in the country by the 1890s, and it held a position of some power in the boot and shoe industry. The practice of 'basket-work' and the use of cheap country labour were strongly opposed and the union demanded that factories should be set up in the villages. Again, the demands of the Boot and Shoe Operatives Union probably contributed to the concentration of the industry in Leicester when, in 1895, a demand was made for an end to the link between factories in the city and country outworkers, a demand that 'all work cut in Leicester shall be made and finished in Leicester'.

In the second half of the 20th century engineering has eclipsed the older Leicestershire industries of hosiery and footwear. There were 7,000 workers in the engineering trades in 1911, and in the same year more than 50,000 were employed in hosiery and boots and shoes. An industrial survey of 1967 showed that almost 70,000 were engaged in engineering; the textile mills found work for 56,000 while scarcely more than 16,000 were employed in footwear. As Dr. Peter Mounfield has written, 'although still important, textiles, clothing and footwear no longer dominate the employment structure in the way they did in 1948, and it is mainly the rapid growth of the engineering industries that has prevented the appearance of what otherwise might have been a significant unemployment problem'.

Engineering was a late-comer on the industrial scene. Early 19th-century trade directories reveal the presence of 'iron-founders' in Leicester. It is believed that the opening of the Soar Navigation, in 1794, with the ability to import cheap coal and pig iron, gave a stimulus to this new industry. James and Benjamin Court, often described as the fathers of engineering in Leicester, established the Britannia Iron Works at Belgrave Gate Wharf. By the 1820s they were busy in the manufacture of metal parts of knitting frames, mile-posts, gratings and the first gas-lamp standards. By the 1840s engineering proper, the designing and making of machines, had truly arrived. A Leicester firm, Pegg and Mason Brothers, was producing machinery and tools for the granite

Leicester clock tower

95

quarries on the flanks of Charnwood Forest. The Phoenix Foundry of William Richards was turning out heavy castings for bridge-building – a firm that flourished on contracts for the new railways. But the engineering industry came to maturity only in the 1870s. Then the iron-founders and tool makers 'ceased to be the handmaiden of hosiery and footwear'. Large firms that sought out markets all over Britain and in the world beyond came into being with products that had nothing to do with Leicestershire's traditional occupations. In 1878, the Vulcan Works was founded on a site covering three acres. In 1872 T.J. Gent had set up as an electrical engineer, though the advance to a large scale in this branch of engineering was to take place at Loughborough where the Brush Company came to specialise in generators, motors, power distribution equipment and electric locomotives. In Leicester the century closed with the foundation of the city's largest engineering works when the partnership of Pearson and Bennion, producing boot and shoe machinery, merged with American interests to form the British United Shoe Machinery Company in 1899. They rose to a monopolist position in this branch of the engineering trades and by the 1930s employed 5,000 workers. Now almost every branch of engineering may be found in Leicester – a diversity of industry that has largely saved the city from the economic depressions and trade slumps of 20th-century Britain.

Market Harborough Town Hall

40. The level crossing at Long Lane on the Leicester and Swannington Railway that gave rise to Coalville, the county's Victorian 'new town'.

41. Bagworth Incline: the cable-hauled section of the Leicester and Swannington Railway in its earliest years whose lower section is now drowned by a large pool formed as a result of mining subsidence.

42. Leicestershire's first canal, 1778: a one-and-a-half-mile-long canal joined the wharf at Loughborough to the river Soar that had been improved and made navigable.

43. The flooded pastures of the Soar at Mountsorrel after several days of heavy summer rainfall.

44. The Moat, Ulverscroft Priory, Charnwood Forest.

45. The London to Leeds motorway, opened in the 1960s, reaches its highest point in Leicestershire in Charnwood Forest.

46. Leicester architect Joseph Goddard's Clock Tower of 1868 stands at the heart of the city close
by the site of the former medieval East Gate. On its lower stage statues of Simon de Montfort,
William Wyggeston, Sir Thomas White, and Alderman Newton recall some of the notable names in
the borough's history. Behind is the Haymarket shopping centre and theatre of the 1970s.

XVI Charnwood Forest

The scenery of Charnwood Forest is strikingly different from any other part of the countryside of Leicestershire and Rutland. The distinctive character of this landscape is owing partly to its physical make-up and to its experience in history. The ancient rocks of Charnwood, reckoned among some of the oldest in the British Isles, outcrop in the rough, craggy skylines of the highest parts of the Forest. The height of the land, modest as it is with the highest point in Leicestershire, Bardon Hill, failing by a few score feet to reach the thousand-foot contour, contributes to the individuality of the region. From Beacon Hill, the windy brow of Old John above Bradgate Park, or any other of the ridges of Charnwood, a wide expanse of Midland countryside lies at one's feet. But the face of this landscape, as seen today, owes much to an event in history that happened less than 200 years ago. An act of parliament for the enclosure of 11,000 acres of the forest was passed in 1808; the completion of the terms of the award was not achieved until 1829. To these two decades at the start of the 19th century are owing many of the details of the present landscape – the pattern of fields, hedged in the richer valleys and walled in dark local stone on the flanks of the rock-strewn ridges – the scattered farmhouses and the mansions of Leicester's industrial magnates, the rectangular shapes of planted spinneys.

Several misconceptions have grown up around the term Charnwood Forest. Hardest to dispel among the many who have written about its history and topography is the view that Charnwood ranked among the great medieval hunting preserves subject to the code of Forest Laws introduced at the time of the Norman Conquest – laws that prohibited the expansion of settlement within the forests, strictly controlled the cutting of timber for fuel, fencing and house building and, above all, limited the hunting of game to certain persons and periods of the year. In this latter part of the 20th century when 'conservation' is an everyday expression, the harsh implications of the Norman forest laws perhaps make a little more sense than they did to our Victorian forefathers. The only part of Leicestershire that was subject to the forest law was the Royal Forest of Leicestershire and Rutland, an extensive tract of woodland that straddled the border of the two counties. Leicester Forest, a woodland tract that stretched from the western precinct of the borough towards Earl Shilton was the property of the Earls of Leicester until the middle of the 13th century; afterwards it formed part of the estates of the Duchy of Lancaster. There is no evidence that Charnwood was ever

St Paul, Woodhouse Eaves, 1837, crowns the rocky face of an abandoned slate quarry

such a royal forest, though some have speculated that such might have been its status before the Norman Conquest. From the 13th century onwards it was divided between the lords of the encircling manors. As George F. Farnham, in his meticulous exploration of Leicestershire's documentary history has written, 'the Forest of Charnwood was a chance concentration of the wastes of the four great manors of Groby, Barrow, Whitwick and Shepshed, together with a small portion of the Loughborough manor waste'.

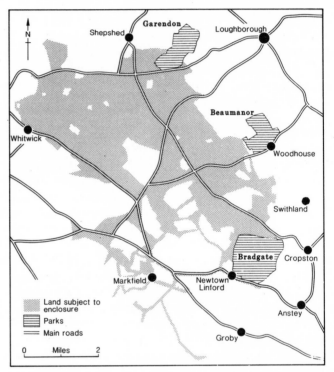

13. Charnwood Forest: enclosure.

If the term 'forest' in the regional name, Charnwood Forest, lacks any legal connotations one might ask whether it has any descriptive value. Certainly the patches of woodland that add beauty to Charnwood's present landscape are mainly the work of the landowners of estates carved out of the former commons after the Enclosure Act of 1808. Any semblance of a forest landscape that the traveller might find in Charnwood today is the work of the Victorians. Scraps of evidence in late medieval documents show that the hills and valleys of Charnwood were once extensively forested. Leland, the first of the great topographers, who travelled the length and breadth of England gathering information about the country's store of antiquities for Henry VIII, described Charnwood as having 'plentye of Woode'. Somewhat earlier than Leland's

98

brief comment on the landscape of Charnwood, the will of Thomas Cotton, who died at Mapplewell in 1507, mentions 300 acres of wood there. But the 16th-century references to Charnwood suggest that this was anything but an unbroken forest at that time. In 1558 a commission was set up to investigate the rights of the priory that had been dissolved at Ulverscroft 20 years earlier. The last of the sub-priors, Thomas Massey, was aged 65 at the time when the commission met. He told them that Ulverscroft possessed timber-cutting rights in Charnwood and they grazed 300 cattle, 1,000 sheep and 60 swine in the 'wastes' of the forest. Thomas Massey added that 'the said priors, during all his time there, have kept hounds, greyhounds and hawks of their own, and did hunt, course and hawk, throughout the waste of Charnwood, unto the saulte of the parks of Bradgate, Groby and Loughborough'. Grazing animals, especially sheep, do not imply healthy, mature woodland, particularly as the prior's flock of 1,000 sheep was not the only one with rights in the unfenced wilderness of Charnwood. All the surrounding manors took their livestock up into the forest for the summer months. By the time of the enclosure, 26 neighbouring villages and hamlets claimed rights of common in Charnwood.

Post-enclosure farm, Charnwood Forest

Even in the early years of the 16th century, before the dissolution of Ulverscroft Priory, there is evidence that the timber resources of the forest were already scarce. Another witness before the commission, Robert Conyngham, claimed that there was hardly sufficient wood in the district to supply the everyday needs of the priory throughout the year. Conyngham reported that 'the whole topwood and underwood growing upon the said wastes and hills were scarce sufficient to suffice the kitchen, brewhouse, bakehouse and other offices of the said house, and for hedging the said closes'. We cannot know the exact route followed by Leland in his journey through Leicestershire, but it is possible that he could have reported on the forest from the chief medieval road between Derby and Leicester that followed the line of the present A6 along the Soar valley. There is good evidence that this has always been the well-wooded flank of the forest. To the west and out of sight of the traveller along that medieval road through Mountsorrel lay thousands of acres of open common land, a landscape of rough pasture, thickets of gorse, blackberry and bracken, and an occasional isolated, gnarled tree such as the one that gave its name to Copt Oak long before the post-enclosure church was raised there in 1837.

By the end of the 18th century Charnwood Forest had been largely stripped of its timber. The records preserve details of the sale of wood to ironmasters in Whitwick and Melbourne for the making of charcoal. In 1673 William Herrick sold to Humphrey Jennens, the Birmingham ironmaster, 6,090 oak and ash trees 'within Beaumanor Liberty on the Forest of Charnwood for the sum of £1, 178'. Again, Nichols reports in his voluminous *History and Antiquities of the County of Leicester* that large quantities of oak from Swithland Wood were sold to the iron founders of Melbourne during the 18th century. The regeneration of woodland within the forest was effectively prevented by grazing sheep and the presence of numerous rabbit warrens. A picture of Charnwood's landscape towards the end of the 18th century is presented in the map of the county published by John Prior in 1779. Prior surveyed the county on a scale of one inch to the mile, producing the first original map of Leicestershire for almost two centuries. On Prior's map, the forest appears as a heathy wilderness that stretches from the bounds of Bradgate Park to the outskirts of Whitwick and Shepshed. The one-inch scale of the survey allowed the depiction of patches of woodland of which there are considerable areas on the eastern flank at Swithland and Beaumanor. Some stands of timber were surviving on the south-western fringe in Steward's Hey and Lea Wood near Groby; the latter name is still alive in a plantation on a slope that steeply overhangs the Ulverscroft valley.

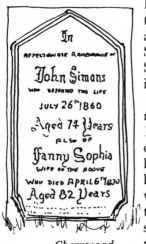

Charnwood slate tombstone

The Act of Enclosure for Charnwood Forest passed through parliament in 1808. Another 20 years elapsed before the distribution of the 11,000 acres of common land between the manorial lords and many other claimants was fully determined. At the outset almost 11,000 acres had to be passed into individual ownership. Altogether 3,800 claims to land in the Forest were submitted. To satisfy all the submitted claims would have required some 60,000 acres – a tract of land more than five times the area of Charnwood. In the end, after patches of land had been set aside for three new churches and the quarries and sheep-washing places allotted to parishes, 8,170 acres were left to satisfy almost 4,000 claims. The award gave 939 acres to the Earl of Stamford, and the largest claim after the Earl's was that of Mr. March Phillipps who received 642 acres on the northern edge of the forest.

Through the place-names and objects in the landscape of Charnwood Forest the work of the 19th-century estate owners can be traced. Thomas Gisborne, a lawyer by profession, planted the woods, Gisborne's Gorse, that encircle the house, Charnwood Lodge. Gisborne employed the skills of a Derbyshire man, Thomas Frith, to transform his section of the common open land into a clearly marked boundary. Frith also built the dry-stone walls that encircle the spinneys in Bradgate Park. Charles Allsop provided an early model for the management of land in Charnwood. As Potter reports, 'his successful exertions excited emulation among other farmers, and gave them assurance that their labours would be crowned with success, by showing them that the wilderness could be turned into a fruitful field; and it may be questioned whether many of the best cultivated farms would have reached their present respectable state of cultivation, but for the example of Mr. Allsop'.

In *The History and Antiquities of Charnwood Forest*, published in 1842, T.R. Potter writes of a Charnwood very different from that of the present day. Much has happened since the 1840s to modify the landscape. The valleys are no longer 'filled with luxuriant corn', but instead there are rough pastures, abandoned and overgrown pits where slate quarrying ceased almost 100 years ago, and numerous blocks and patches of planted woodland on the sites of fields that were ploughed for corn

100

crops in the early years of the enclosure. The long years of agricultural depression in the last quarter of the 19th century hit the new farms of Charnwood Forest severely. On the attractive southern fringe of the region, within close reach of Leicester, estates were sold to the rich industrialists of the borough. Allsop's Victorian successors were able to apply the principles of landscape gardening, as he did, and went further in the aesthetic management of the landscape with the planting of a great variety of exotic species among which the acres of rhododendron are now so evident.

The place names of the Forest lack the sound of a deep past – Greenhill Lodge, Blackbird's Nest and Rock Farm, for example – but have the more matter-of-fact tones of the 19th century. Some names commemorate the first owners of estates created by the enclosure. Bess Bagley Farm, near Copt Oak, bears the same name as Mrs. Elizabeth Baggerley – a name that is marked against the owner of this property on the enclosure award map. Even so, a scattering of much older place names has survived to recall the Forest's medieval centuries. Ulverscroft, Ulf's farm, is named for a settler from Scandinavia, or at least his descendant, from the time before the foundation of an Augustinian priory in this quiet valley early in the 12th century. Alderman Haw, Sheet Hedges, Copt Oak and Timber Wood are among the contemporary place names that are already recorded in the 14th century. Much has happened to Charnwood's landscape since the enclosure. The quarrying for road metal gnaws at its ancient rocks, the gift of Bradgate Park to the city and county has fossilised a fragment of the older pre-enclosure landscape and early in the 1960s the making of England's first motorway, the M1, sliced through the heart of this region whose road patterns had been undisturbed since the enclosure commissioners did their work.

Charnwood Forest – general view

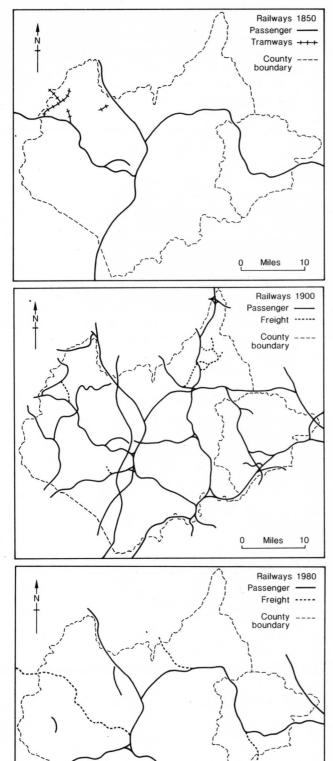

14. The early railway network shows the role of the Soar valley and the Leicestershire coalfield in the development of this revolutionary means of transport before 1850. By 1900, competition between rival companies had laced the Leicestershire landscape with a network of lines (note the freight railways in the northeast that opened up the iron-ore fields towards the close of the 19th century). The surviving railways of 1980 make a map that closely resembles that of 1850.

XVII Railways and the Landscape

Leicestershire occupies a special place in Britain's railway history because one of the earliest lines operated by steam-powered locomotives, the Leicester and Swannington, was opened for goods and passenger traffic by the summer of 1832. At the time of its opening there were only five other railways in Britain employing steam locomotives and that were engaged in public transport. Ten years later, when the Midland Railway was taking shape, Leicestershire found itself strategically placed across several projected routes between London and the north, and during the latter part of the 19th century the East Midland countryside became the scene of intense conflict between competing railway companies.

Although the Leicester and Swannington represents one of the great landmarks in the technological revolution brought about by the railways, it was not the first attempt to improve the transport of coal from the Leicestershire coalfield by loaded wagons running along fixed tracks. The broken landscape of west Leicestershire on the northern fringe of Charnwood Forest provided a severe obstacle in the way of canal building. The Charnwood Forest Canal, designed to ease the movement of coal to the wharfs of the Soar Navigation at Loughborough, involved the construction of a two-and-three-quarter mile length of railway at an average gradient of 1 in 78 between the canal terminal at Nanpantan and Loughborough. This railway, completed in 1794, fell out of use after the frosts and floods of the severe winter of 1799 had damaged the earthworks of the canal and burst the feeder reservoir at Blackbrook. Many years later, in the 1880s, this 18th-century railway link between the Charnwood Forest Canal and the Soar became part of the London and North Western's line across the coalfield from Nuneaton to Loughborough. By 1802 the Ashby Canal had penetrated the western flank of the coalfield. Access to the coalpits and limestone quarries lying to the north and east of Ashby de la Zouch was secured by the construction of tramways that focused on the canal basin at Willesley. The main tramway, using horse-drawn wagons, led for eight-and-a-half miles by Ashby de la Zouch to the limestone quarries at Ticknall. From the 'wharf' – the name given to the loading points on the earliest railways – at the eastern end of Old Parks Tunnel a branch line extended for four miles to the collieries at Lount and the lime works of Breedon Cloud. The tramway worked until the middle years of the 19th century. Later, in 1874, the Midland Railway rebuilt the section from Ashby to the Breedon quarries as part of a branch line between Derby and Ashby de la Zouch.

The creation of the Leicester and Swannington Railway arose from a meeting of colliery owners and local traders at the *Bell Hotel*, Leicester, on 12 February 1829. The main purpose was to find a means of widening the market for Leicestershire coal through a reduction in the costs of transport out of the coalfield to provide effective competition in the borough with the water-borne coal from Derbyshire. The idea of a railway had developed in the mind of William Stenson, a colliery owner of Whitwick, who had seen the Stockton and Darlington Railway at work in 1828. John Ellis, a wealthy Leicester Quaker, was the other leading name in the promotion of the railway. Ellis was a friend of George Stephenson, and perhaps it was this personal link, above all else, that first brought this revolutionary system of transport from its birthplace in the north of England to the Midlands. George Stephenson's son, Robert, a young man in his 20s, was appointed engineer for the railway into the coalfield. Stephenson's connections with businessmen in Liverpool helped to find capital for the building of the line, though it should be remembered that two-thirds of the original sum of £90,000 was raised locally in Leicester and the county.

The problems of the first railway engineers are well represented in the layout of the Leicester and Swannington. Only the most gentle gradients could be tackled by the primitive steam locomotives. Consequently the climb from the terminus on the bank of the Soar at West Bridge into the broken countryside on the western flank of Charnwood Forest involved the piercing of the sandstone ridge at Glenfield by a tunnel of more than one mile in length. The narrow bore of the tunnel reflects the dimensions of the coaches and wagons of the period. The later passenger coaches that used the line until it was closed in 1928 had their windows barred for the safety of passengers that might be tempted to put their heads out. Guards' vans were built with inward opening doors should the need arise for an official to leave the train inside the tunnel. The final accounts of the Leicester and Swannington Railway show that the building of the tunnel cost much more than the projected sum of £90,000. The accounts show that the Glenfield tunnel overran the estimate by more than £7,000. The increased cost of cutting the tunnel was explained by the need for a brick lining throughout its length. Trial borings had shown that the tunnel would run mainly through solid rock; instead, the engineers encountered 500 yards of unstable sand.

Keeper's cottage, Bagworth

The limited power of the early locomotives – 10 were employed on the railway in the 1830s – meant that long, steep gradients demanded greater sources of power. Two considerable changes of height interrupted the smooth running of the Leicester and Swannington Railway. One, the Bagworth Incline, rose in a short distance through more than 100 feet to the west of Thornton. The other, the Swannington Incline, descended sharply through 150 feet over a distance of half-a-mile to the

104

coal pits at the end of the line. The Bagworth Incline, with a gradient of 1 in 29, was worked by a cable around a pulley at the top of the incline. The loaded coal trucks, bound for Leicester, hauled up the empties, and passengers were compelled to walk this part of their journey. Soon after the Midland Railway took over the Leicester and Swannington, in 1847, the stiff gradient at Bagworth was replaced by a gentler diversion that allowed unbroken working to the head of the Swannington Incline. The descent into the coalfield at Swannington, with a gradient of 1 in 17, was worked by a stationary steam engine at its head, an engine that was designed by Robert Stephenson. The haulage of coal wagons on the Swannington Incline with its stationary engine ceased only in 1948, but for many years traffic had been light. Even at the completion of the incline in 1833 the focus of activity in the Leicestershire coalfield was already moving south to the richer deeply buried seams at Ibstock, Ellistown and Bagworth where the numerous colliery branch lines to the Leicester and Swannington Railway were an important factor in the development of the concealed coalfield.

Leicestershire's first railway was created out of the demands of the coal trade; passenger traffic played little part in its operations. Figures of receipts for the first six months of 1843 show that passenger fares accounted for only 5.1 per cent of the railway's takings. In the same period as many as 3,000 wagons of coal were handled at the West Bridge terminus. The effect of the new railway on coal prices in Leicester was startling. The price of Derbyshire coal, brought into the borough by the Soar Navigation, was cut by more than seven shillings a ton – more than one third of the cost of that coal on the wharfs at Leicester. One month after the opening of the Leicester and Swannington, the Derbyshire colliery owners met at the *Sun Inn*, Eastwood, where they resolved 'to lay a railway from these collieries to the town of Leicester'. Thus, the demands and rivalries of the coal trade were to bring into being the Midland Counties Railway.

In 1844, the Midland Railway Company was formed out of three systems focused on Derby – the Midland Counties Railway, The Birmingham and Derby Junction Railway and the North Midland Railway. The Act of Parliament that allowed this amalgamation of the three railways was the first step in the evolution of a national railway network. Birmingham, Rugby, Leicester, Nottingham, Derby, Sheffield and Leeds were served by one railway company. Leicestershire belonged to the south-eastern limb of the Midland system. The Midland Counties Railway began a regular service of trains between Leicester and Nottingham in the early summer of 1840 over a route that had been laid without any major obstacles along the Soar valley. Although the impetus for the building of the railway had come from the colliery owners of Derbyshire, the planning of the Midland Counties was strongly influenced by individuals far removed from the Leicestershire scene. Much of the capital came from investors in Liverpool who saw the Midland Counties Railway as part of an evolving national system – a new means

*Glenfield
tunnel, now
sealed*

of communication that was to extinguish the stage coach and successfully threaten the canals in the traffic of heavy goods. Liverpool's investors determined that the Midland Counties should continue beyond Leicester, to Rugby where a link could be made with the London and Birmingham Railway that had opened in 1838.

Two years after the incorporation of the Midland, in 1846, the Leicester and Swannington was purchased. The takeover of Leicestershire's first railway was a symptom of the intense rivalry that arose between railway promoters in the 1840s and that was to be an important factor in railway history for the rest of the 19th century. The cause of the Midland's interest in the Leicester and Swannington was a scheme, put forward in 1845, for the formation of a Leicester and Bedford Railway Company whose lines would link up with the London and York Railway (later the Great Northern working out of King's Cross). By this route across the South Midlands coal from the Swannington line could reach London. Such an arrangement threatened to stifle the traffic along the Midland's own outlet to London through Rugby and along the tracks of the London and Birmingham Railway (later that great national company, the London and North Western). Like many schemes of the years of the Railway Mania in 1845 and 1846 the Leicester and Bedford Railway came to nothing. It was not until 1857, and then at the hands of the Midland, that a route from Wigston, on the Leicester-Rugby line, opened to Bedford and Hitchin where access into the Great Northern's line into London was achieved. A decade later, in 1868, the Midland completed its own entry into the capital city with the opening of the line from Bedford to St Pancras. Leicester's first main line to London – the only one that survives today – was a quarter of a century in the making and pieced together from three different railway projects.

Within the county the advent of the Midland Railway Company in the 1840s was to have important social consequences. The Leicester and Swannington Railway was primarily a carrier of coal; with the Midland the movement of passengers became important. Previously the Leicester and Swannington had left the handling of passenger traffic to hotels close to the coal railway. At Long Lane, known as Coalville by 1835, there were no railway buildings; business was carried on at the *Railway Hotel*. By 1848 the Midland had opened a passenger station there – the first step in the making of a Victorian new town at the heart of the Leicestershire coalfield. In 1846 and 1847 the directors of the Midland obtained Acts of Parliament that were to transform the Leicester and Swannington into a regional railway – a trunk line through west Leicestershire. An extension from Coalville to Burton-on-Trent to join the Midland's main route between Derby and Birmingham was allowed, a line from Desford to Knighton gave direct access to the Midland station at Campbell Street in Leicester, and a diversion was built to the Bagworth Incline that permitted the through-running of trains.

The railway entrepreneurs of Victorian England found themselves in a very different territory when they turned their eyes towards east

Leicestershire and Rutland. A countryside of big estates and small scattered rural communities offered little incentive for the growth of railway traffic. The scarped ridges and valleys of this landscape, the watershed between streams draining to the Trent and the Wash, presented the most difficult topography in the East Midlands to the railway engineers. Again, in this territory of the famous hunts the railway builders met a powerful social hostility. Consequently, the railway age in the East Midlands belongs largely to the last quarter of the 19th century. The main incentive to the promotion of railways in the territory to the east of Leicester lay in the rivalry and competition that the railway companies generated between themselves. Among the region's limited resources only the prospect of opening up the iron ore deposits to the north-east of Melton Mowbray held out strong hope of profit. The first railway into east Leicestershire and Rutland came with the fierce expansion of the Midland in the 1840s. Within months of the formation of the railway, a line was planned between Syston and Peterborough. The chief aim of this line was to forestall the advances of the London and York Railway into the unclaimed territory of the East Midlands. By 1845 an act of parliament had been obtained for a winding route that followed the Wreake and Chater valleys joining together the small market towns of Melton Mowbray, Oakham and Stamford.

Brooksby station on the Midland Railway's branch from Syston to Peterborough

The social hostility of the hunting country to the first railways is recorded in the scuffles that took place between the agents of Lord Harborough on his estate at Stapleford and the surveyors and navvies of the railway company. Harborough's efforts to keep the railway away from his estate, in addition to the threats which the Midland presented to the Oakham Canal in which he was a major shareholder, delayed the opening of the middle section of the line between Melton Mowbray and Oakham for two years. The diversion of the tracks from the edge of Stapleford Park involved the construction of a sharp curve at Saxby, known to this day as Lord Harborough's Curve. Half a century later, its sharpness became an obstacle in the express timetables of the newly opened direct line between Nottingham and St Pancras. The Midland Railway secured an agreement with Lord Harborough's descendant for a new diversion and easier curve close by the edge of Stapleford Park.

The era of railway building in east Leicestershire began only in the 1870s when the four chief companies of the central Midlands, fearing each other's activities, found reason to promote schemes. The Great Northern, whose main line skirted the edge of Rutland between Peterborough and Grantham, sought access to Leicester. The London and North Western, whose main line touched the western fringe of Leicestershire to the north of Rugby, wanted to tap the coal traffic of the Nottinghamshire coalfield and wanted to find a terminus in the county town as well. The Manchester, Sheffield and Lincolnshire Railway, to be renamed the Great Central at the turn of the century, looked across the borderland of Leicestershire and Rutland in its search for a possible route to London. All the companies with an interest in this territory realised that the iron

107

ore reserves near Melton Mowbray would provide an important source of traffic.

Rivalry rather than sound economic reasoning lay behind the railway investment of the late 19th century. As P. Howard Anderson has written in his book, *Forgotten Railways*, 'one of the last considerations in the minds of promoters was to provide transport for isolated villages or solitary upland farms'. After complex arrangements between the Great Northern and the London and North Western and much lobbying in parliament, as well as opposition from the hunting gentry, the plans for a railway across the difficult terrain of east Leicestershire from Newark to Market Harborough were laid. Branches were to be thrown off for the Great Northern to a terminus in Belgrave Road, Leicester, and for the London and North Western into Nottingham. The line ran across the grain of the county, a spectacular route through an unspectacular landscape with many expensive tunnels, viaducts, embankments and cuttings. At Scalford, to the north of Melton Mowbray, a system of mineral lines reached into the iron ore fields of Eaton and Holwell.

Seaton viaduct carried the Midland Railway across the Welland valley on 82 arches

The joint railway of the Great Northern and London and North Western across east Leicestershire opened in 1879; the branch to the terminus at Belgrave Road, Leicester, was completed by 1882. This 'impresssive terminus' with its five platforms under a twin-arched roof 'represented the triumphant entry of the Great Northern Railway into another Midland Railway stronghold'. The Midland was not slow to take up the challenge of the Great Northern's entry into Leicestershire. In 1875 they placed a scheme before parliament for a direct route between Nottingham and Kettering which involved the building of only two sections of railway to link up with the existing tracks of the Syston and Peterborough line between Melton Mowbray and Manton. On 1 June 1880, the first direct Midland expresses between Nottingham and St Pancras opened up this route, a line that overcame the topographical obstacles with nine tunnels in the space of 50 miles between Nottingham and Kettering. The Manchester, Sheffield and Lincolnshire Railway had speculated upon the idea of a main line southwards to the capital across east Leicestershire, but when their plans came to fruition in the closing years of the 19th century, the thrust southwards from Nottingham took in Loughborough, Leicester and Rugby to enter London in a new terminus at Marylebone from the north-west. At the opening of its main line to London in 1899, the Manchester, Sheffield and Lincolnshire took on the grandiloquent name of the Great Central – not without some justification, for this last of the great main lines had been designed with all the insight acquired in three-quarters of a century of railway engineering. Long straight sections, gentle curves and easy gradients made for fast running. The 27 miles between Leicester and Nottingham were regularly covered in 23 minutes. The Great Central reached the two Midland cities at enormous expense – Nottingham by tunnels and deep cuttings, Leicester across a mile-long viaduct of 96 arches and 16 girder bridges.

The network of the county's railways was complete by the beginning of the 20th century. Scarcely more than half a century later only one passenger route survived to the east of the Soar – the tracks of the earliest railway in east Leicestershire and Rutland, the Syston and Peterborough. One main line – the Midland along the Soar valley – bears all the long-distance traffic. The Great Central is reduced to five miles of single track between Loughborough Central and Rothley over which the enthusiastic, unpaid members of *The Main Line Steam Trust* run engines, rescued from distant parts of the British railway system, at weekends.

From a frieze on the former offices of Thomas Cook commemorating the historic first organised excursion by railway in July, 1841

XVIII Leicester in the Nineteenth Century

Leicester's population statistics, gathered at the beginning of each decade through the 19th century, reveal the importance of the Victorian years in the making of the town. The hundred years between 1801 and 1901 saw a 12-fold increase in the population of the borough. At the beginning of the century Leicester had 17,000 inhabitants; by 1841 the numbers had grown to 40,000 and at the end of Victoria's reign there were 212,000 living within the much extended bounds of the former medieval town.

Victoria came to the throne in 1837; by that year several of the characteristic institutions of the Victorian town were already in existence. Of high importance were the changes wrought by two political acts of central government early in the 1830s. In 1835 Lord John Russell introduced a bill in parliament that provided for the radical reconstruction of the corporations of 183 towns. Under its terms, town councillors were to be elected for three years by ratepayers of three years' standing. The elections to the new town council of Leicester that followed on 26 December 1835 put an end to the old order of local government. Three years before the demise of the old corporation it had been subjected to a visitation of two commissioners inquiring into the municipal corporations in the Midland Circuit. The corporation, they reported, 'had great wealth, yet did little to ease public burdens' and admission to civic office rested in membership of the corporation party.

The reformed corporation that took office in the last week of 1835 set the pattern of Leicester's local politics for the rest of the century. Radical Leicester, the nickname that became attached to the borough, derived from this revolution in local government. In the election of 1835 the victory of the Liberals was complete. Out of 42 councillors, only four of those were returned as Tories. The new councillors were mostly industrialists and vocal members of the several dissenting chapels. One place of worship, the Unitarian Great Meeting, exerted an immense influence in the affairs of the new corporation. On New Year's Day, 1836, Thomas Paget was elected and sworn in as mayor. He was the first of seven successive mayors who came from the Great Meeting. The new corporation's streak of nonconformist puritanism helped it to dismiss the last faded symbols of the Middle Ages from local government in its efforts to liquidate a debt of more than £20,000 inherited from the old order. Now the new broom swept through the offices of the corporation. The posts of mace-bearer, sergeants-at-mace – all four of them: town crier, two bellmen, six town waits, beadle and mole catcher – all were

17th-century mace

110

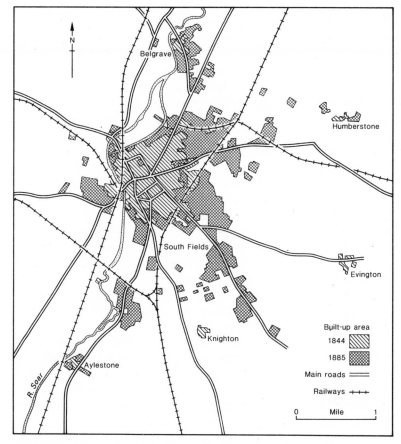

15. The expansion of Leicester in the 19th century.

abolished. The town's great mace, acquired in the 17th century, was put up to auction along with 62 acres of corporation land. Civic feasts, an ancient perquisite of members of the old corporation, were abolished and the large stocks of plate, cutlery, glass and linen were sold. After five years the last debt inherited from the old corporation had been paid off.

An equally important transformation of the political life of the borough was brought about by the Reform Act of 1832 which abruptly changed the character of Leicester's representation in parliament. The Reform Act extended the franchise in towns to all of the £10 householders; non-resident freemen who had previously played an important part in borough elections were deprived of the vote. As a result, Leicester remained a stronghold of liberalism in parliamentary politics until the end of the 19th century.

The Great Meeting

Leicester grew steadily through the first half of the 19th century. A population of less than 20,000 in 1800 reached almost 70,000 by 1860. William Cobbett, in his *Rural Rides* published in 1830, has left a vivid

111

Leicester Museum

impression of the town at the outset of its decades of Victorian expansion. 'Leicester is a very fine town,' he commented, 'spacious streets, fine inns, fine shops, and containing, they say, thirty or forty thousand people.' But Cobbett makes clear that Leicester was still in essence a country market town separated by an unspoilt countryside from its rim of surrounding villages – Belgrave, Evington, Knighton, Wigston and Aylestone. 'Standing on the hill at Knighton, you see the three ancient and lofty and beautiful spires rising up at Leicester; you see the river winding down through a broad bed of the most beautiful meadows that man ever set his eyes on'. A century later, Leicester's rural ring where Cobbett found villages whose spires rose up 'amongst the trees in the dells, at scarcely ever more than a mile or two apart' had been overrun by the factories, railway tracks, terraced housing, cemeteries, parks and scrapyards of the Victorian city.

The growth of Leicester between 1840 and 1860 served two different social purposes and fulfilled the demands of two different classes in her population. There was the need to house the rising working class of labourers and artisans employed in the dominant hosiery industry and there was a fashionable demand for comfortable houses outside the core of the old borough that arose from the wealth of the middle class. Land for the physical expansion of the town was available in the hundreds of acres of former open fields that encircled Leicester to east and south. The East Field, enclosed and in private ownership since 1764, had provided land for speculative buildings since the end of the 18th century. From the South Field, largely in the possession of the corporation since its enclosure in 1811, plots of building land were sold off in the 1830s to meet the debts left behind by the old corporation.

The bricks and mortar of the expanding town spread across the pastures of the East Field in the first half of the 19th century. By 1830 the ancient core of the borough – within the line of the vanished medieval wall – was flanked by a new residential suburb largely occupied by the working classes. Ellis's map of 1828 shows the whole area between the canal and as far east as the present-day Abbey Park Road as completely built up; further close development is focused on Wharf Street and Rutland Street – the latter a thoroughfare whose name had been lately changed from Dogkennel Lane, a symptom of the vanishing rural rim around the borough. The expansion of the eastern margin of the town is marked by the building of St George's church in 1827, the first parish created in Leicester since the early Middle Ages, and the forerunner of a succession of Victorian churches that split the vast medieval parish of St Margaret's into 10 separate parishes before the end of the 19th century. The opening of the Midland Counties Railway in 1840, its tracks skirting the flanks of the town through the former South and East Fields, provided a further incentive to the development of this quarter. Between 1850 and 1860 more than 500 houses were put up along the Humberstone Road alone. A large new residential suburb of poor quality housing had come into being by the middle of the century. The problems of inadequate

Decoration from Town Hall Square fountain

112

sanitation and water supply led to severe outbreaks of cholera, typhus and smallpox. In 1849 more than half of the streets were without sewers and the water supply of the borough came from some 6,000 wells and cisterns, many of them reaching down to a water table polluted by sewage. In the 1840s, Leicester's death rate of 30 per 1,000 was only capped by Bristol, Liverpool and Manchester. It was one of the unhealthiest places in the British Isles.

The Victoria Coffee House, Granby Street, Leicester, opened 1888

A second, though less extensive, area of poor housing arose along the east bank of the Soar reaching out to the Welford Road and the sites of the infirmary and the prison. Here working class housing intermingled with warehouses and workshops of hosiers and the premises of the growing boot and shoe industry. It is evident that during the first part of the 19th century much land remained unoccupied by buildings in the heart of the town. William Gardiner, in his book *Music and Friends, or Pleasant Recollections of a Dilettante*, published in 1838, presents a vivid account of his native town in those years. To the north of High Street, reaching as far as Sanvey Gate on the line of the former town wall, was a patchwork of gardens and orchards. William Gardiner remembers this 'vacant ground enclosed in every direction by walls made of mud and straw, forming dark and gloomy lanes'. He records the changes that were afoot in this quarter of the borough. 'Within the last twenty years the mud walls have begun to disappear and houses for working people give a more cheerful aspect to this solitary part of the town.' The latter half of the 19th century brought even more drastic changes to this part of Leicester's townscape. Here the factories and warehouses of the borough's late industrial revolution pressed close to the heart of the old town. The traffic needs of the 20th century have largely obliterated the objects of the Victorian scene – mills and houses and the narrow streets and cul-de-sacs that followed the lines of the ancient lanes between gardens and orchards. Today the inner ring road sweeps through this segment of the inner city with its parking lots and multi-storey car park.

Much of the visual character of modern Leicester derives from the years between 1860 and 1914. The 1860s saw a sudden rise in the population of the borough, a rapid rate of growth that was maintained until the end of the century. Between 1861 and 1871 Leicester's population increased by 40 per cent. It was the highest recorded rate of growth among the 20 largest towns of the United Kingdom. For the next 30 years the borough increased its population by one-third of the total in each decade. The boom years of the '60s, as Leicester embraced the new machines and factories in hosiery, boots and shoes and engineering, are vividly recorded in the annual reports of Joseph Dare, a minister of Great Meeting whose domestic mission worked in the new suburbs of Victorian Leicester. In 1863, a time of rising prosperity, he recorded 'with the increase of population, we are fast losing the character of a quiet inland town . . . wine shops, cigar divans, casinos, and public house dancing rooms, are springing up in all parts of the town, offering temptations to spend money without profit, and alluring the thoughtless to degradation and ruin'.

113

The 19th century saw a great expansion in the educational facilities of the city. By 1836 only a few pupils still attended the old Free Grammar School. A private school – the Collegiate School – was established, but the decision to appoint only Anglicans to the staff meant that nonconformists were effectively excluded. Members of the various dissenting groups of Leicester joined together to found their own school, but it failed to attract pupils in sufficient numbers, and closed in 1847. The Collegiate School continued as a girls' grammar school until it was merged in a new Sixth Form College system in 1980. Other private schools also appeared, including the Wyggeston Girls' School and the City of Leicester Boys' School. The old grammar school itself was refounded in 1877 in a building which now houses a privately supported secondary school that has taken the name of the Leicester Grammar School. Nevertheless, by 1870 there were only enough places for half the schoolchildren of Leicester, and the corporation was obliged to take a hand in the matter. The city established its first five schools in 1874: they were King Richard's School, Syston Street, Oxford Street, Elbow Lane and Slater Street. Only Slater Street is still used today, but many newer establishments have been set up subsequently.

Between 1861 and 1911 the population of Leicester rose from 68,000 to a little more than a quarter of a million; the built-up town spread widely into the surrounding countryside. By the 1870s 'it was difficult to say where the town ended and the suburban village began'. The most striking development in the growth of the borough during the 1860s was the spread of the town to the west bank of the river Soar. The late expansion of Leicester into the one-time acres of the West Field may owe something to the physical barrier presented by the river and the frequency of its floods, but an even greater deterrent to the town's growth in this direction was the presence of two large estates, Westcotes and Dannet's Hall, that had been carved at an early date out of the territory of the West Field. Both came on to the land market in the 1860s and the way was opened to the speculative builder. This area still bears faint traces of its distinctive late Victorian social character.

Westminster Bank

Leicester's middle-class business community made its own contribution to the shaping of the borough in the latter part of the 19th century. Stoneygate, the suburb that rose along the London Road in the south-eastern fringe of the borough, acquired a snobbish distinctiveness that has outlived its roomy late-Victorian and Edwardian houses with their stabling for carriages and horses. The 20th century has changed Victorian Stoneygate into a suburb of small hotels that provide lodging for business 'reps' and expensive flats that have arisen in the spacious gardens of demolished family houses.

The late Victorian expansion of Leicester with 35,000 houses built between 1860 and the opening years of the 20th century deeply affected local government. The Local Government Act of 1888 raised Leicester to the status of a county borough. In 1891 the Leicester Extension Act recognised the rapid growth of the town that had taken place since the

114

1860s. The new boundaries trebled the area under the control of the corporation. The topographical expansion of urban Leicester out to the surrounding villages was signalled by the absorption of Belgrave, Knighton and Aylestone, as well as parts of Hunberstone, Evington and Braunstone. The political revolution of Leicester continued into the 20th century when the status of city was granted in 1919; and in 1927 the carving of a fresh diocese out of the bishopric of Peterborough was to return Leicester, after more than a thousand years, to the role of a cathedral city.

In the latter part of the 19th century Leicester corporation played an ever-increasing part in the shaping of the life of the borough. Amongst the many schemes of the municipal authority – the widening of roads, the making of parks, a reconstruction of the sewage system in the 1890s, the building of reservoirs – the greatest undertaking during the 19th century was the improvement of the river Soar to contain its floods. The springtime floods of 1867 led the corporation to acquire a succession of acts for the improvement and drainage of the Soar in 1868, 1874, 1876 and 1881. The sluggish run-off of the river had been aggravated by mill-dams and the building of railway embankments. The widening and deepening of the river bed, cutting of new channels, and removal of weirs was completed in 1891. The whole operation cost the borough £300,000 at a time when the rateable value of Leicester was little more than £500,000.

As the nascent city grew outwards in the closing decades of Victoria's reign the townscape of the old borough – the area within the line of the medieval wall – was not without its many changes. New buildings expressed the rising prosperity of the county town. Town Hall Square evolved as a new piece of the urban scene in the 1870s, on the site of the old Horse Fair. The new Town Hall in its warm Suffolk brick with window dressing of pale Ketton stone is notable among the public buildings of Victorian England. A competition for its design awarded the prize to a young Leicester-born architect, F.J. Hames, who also designed the fountain that forms the centrepiece of the Square. Banks recorded the prosperity of late-Victorian Leicester in new, ornate buildings. Joseph Godard, a local architect, designed a building for the Leicester Banking Company, now the Midland, in Granby Street and another Leicester architect, Perkins Pick, built the spacious new headquarters of Pares' Bank, now the central city bank of the National Westminster, in St Martin's. The *Grand Hotel*, completed in 1898, best expresses the mood of those years; it is the very antithesis of those austere buildings that survived from the early years of the century – the New Walk Museum, the Leicestershire and Rutland Asylum, now the University, and the Central Lending Library, in Belvoir Street, originally the Mechanics' Institute and a public assembly hall of 1831. A special feature among the buildings of late Victorian Leicester was created by the temperance movement and the building of a number of coffee houses. The buildings, still standing in the High Street and Granby Street,

*Leicester
Town Hall*

115

shelter the activities of insurance companies and chain stores. But the greatest change in the townscape of the inner city came with the building of the Great Central Railway in 1899. Three hundred houses were destroyed on the western fringe of the old town, a new street, Great Central Street, was made to give access to the new station on its long raised embankment. But the damage to the face of Leicester could have been much worse if the Great Central had been allowed to follow the line of its original plan to the east of the river through the Jewry Wall and the site of the castle. The protests of the local Archaeological Society succeeded in preserving these oldest fragments of the city from the railway builders whose own works, the girder bridges and grey-blue walls of Staffordshire brick, now stand as a memorial to the greatest revolution of the Victorian years, the railways.

Baptist Chapel (the Pork Pie Chapel), Belvoir Street, Leicester, 1845 — now the Adult Education Centre

116.

XIX Twentieth-Century Change

The evolution of Leicestershire and Rutland in the present century is focused on three phases separated by two periods in which Britain has been locked in European wars. The opening years of the century, until the outbreak of World War I in 1914, belong properly to the evening of Victorian England. The inter-war years, between 1919 and 1939, bear some of the main characteristics of the 20th century. They foreshadow the decline of the railways and their replacement by road vehicles as the chief means of transport. The first projects for municipal housing appear in the 1920s to be followed, in the 1930s, with the first efforts towards slum clearance in the big cities. Immense changes in both town and countryside have taken place over the years since World War II. Extensive tracts of the inner city have been rebuilt, a new long-distance transport network has been created with the motorways, and in the countryside the reshaping of field boundaries has introduced a transformation of the landscape and economy only to be matched by the enclosures of the 18th century.

Lutyens' War Memorial in Victoria Park

The closing years of the 19th century were marked in Leicester by the rising importance of local government. The 20th century has continued this trend. In 1935 the area of the city was doubled when a newly defined boundary encompassed Gilroes, Braunstone Frith, New Parks and Beaumont Leys, and large parts of Evington, Humberstone and Braunstone were taken into Leicester. The city council also became an important builder of houses. The first estate for municipal building – the Coleman Road estate in North Evington – was bought in 1919. During the '20s, large municipal housing projects developed to the south and west of Leicester in Saffron Lane and on a 1,000 acre estate at Braunstone. A succession of land deals between 1933 and 1937 prepared the way for another development of municipal house building in the New Parks estate after the Second World War. During the post-war decades, this pattern of local authority housing that had evolved between 1920 and 1939 continued. In those years 12,000 houses were built within the bounds of the city, and of that number three-quarters belonged to the local authority. The remainder were put up largely by speculative builders to the south and east of the city and on its northern fringe. The housing developments of the 20th century have reinforced a division in

117

St Matthew's estate, Leicester

the social geography of Leicester that appeared in the 19th century. Stoneygate, Evington and Knighton have remained the territory of the middle classes, of those who have bought their own homes. To the west of the Soar, a belt of large municipal estates, largely working class, stretches from Braunstone through New Parks to Mowmacre Hill. The growth of Oadby in the 1960s and '70s underlines this trend in the evolution of Leicester and its ring of suburbs. Over a period of 15 years, between 1951 and 1966, Oadby's population grew from 6,200 to 16,300 – almost entirely as a result of speculative building. A survey in 1966 showed that 40 per cent of Oadby's working population belonged to professional and managerial classes, and another 26 per cent was engaged in non-manual jobs.

Leicester's suburban expansion in the 20th century has been matched by a drastic clearance and rebuilding of parts of the inner city. This massive slum clearance, on either side of Belgrave Gate, made way for St Margaret's bus station and the site of the first municipal car-park. The Second World War called a halt to the reshaping of inner Leicester and it was not until the late 1950s that an extensive firmly planned programme of redevelopment began. The transformations of the latter half of the 20th century have removed much of the Victorian town. By 1970 a quarter between Belgrave Road, Humberstone Road and the railway tracks to the north of the Midland Station, a district of mid-Victorian terraced housing, small factories and workshops, had been largely cleared and rebuilt.

Two other quarters of Leicester's inner city have undergone deep changes in the second half of this century. A mid-Victorian industrial district of hosiery factories and streets of terraced housing that stretched southwards from the Newarke towards the Royal Infirmary and west-ward to the river has been largely swept away. Much of the land is now taken up by lecture rooms and laboratories of the Polytechnic and the vastly expanded buildings of the Royal Infirmary. The surgery of the town planner has been equally drastic in its treatment of the quarter lying to the north of the High Street, between Churchgate and Highcross Street. The warehouses and factories that took over the gardens and orchards scarcely more than 100 years ago have now been demolished. Early in the 1970s the Haymarket shopping 'mall' took the place of the inns that had been there since the days of the stagecoach.

Haymarket Centre

The biggest challenge of the 20th century to those in charge of the development of the city has been the motor-car and the need to provide roads for an ever increasing volume of traffic. Leicester's traffic problems were first tackled in the 1920s and '30s – some would argue in a half-hearted and unsatisfactory way. The city's position at the convergence of long-distance routes across the Midlands meant that much traffic between London and the north of England passed through the streets at the centre of the town. By the late 1920s, Leicester had become an important staging point on bus routes between Manchester and London. In 1922 a plan was drawn up for the building of an outer ring road

118

whose course lay for the most part outside the city boundary at that time. Disagreement between Leicester Corporation and neighbouring local councils meant that little was achieved in making the outer ring road in the inter-war years. By 1939 and the outbreak of the Second World War, only short sections, mainly in the new housing estates of the 1930s, had been completed. By the 1980s, the rising traffic between the M1 motorway and the busy ports of East Anglia had brought the need for a diversionary road system around the city to the fore.

The second road project of the 1920s for an inner ring road to move traffic away from Granby Street, Gallowtreegate and Belgrave Gate at the centre of the city met with greater success. A preliminary scheme for a complete inner ring was rejected in 1924. Instead a plan for a dual carriageway was approved. This street, Charles Street, the most important work of the inter-war years in the city, was opened in 1932. The 1960s saw the completion of a road system for fast-moving traffic through the western and northern quarters of the old town. The final squeezing-out of traffic from the heart of Leicester, from streets that lie within the perimeter of the former medieval wall, began in the late 1970s with the exclusion of all vehicles, except bus service and essential shop deliveries, from the centre of the town.

Huntingdon's Tower, sole remainder of the medieval town house of the Earls of Huntingdon

The most striking change in the life of Leicester came about with the influx of immigrants from Commonwealth countries. The first immigrants, in the 1950s, came mainly from the West Indies. Even so, the latest survey of the ethnic origins of the city's population, published in *The Survey of Leicester, 1983*, shows that they form only a small portion, some 1.8 per cent, of the 286,000 inhabitants of Leicester who live within the city boundaries. Incomers from India and Pakistan dominated through the 1960s and together with the Asians from Kenya who came to Britain towards the end of that decade they now number 63,200 or 22.1 per cent of the population. By the early 1970s, the social problems of overcrowding in Highfields and in the streets of Victorian terraces along the Melton Road caused the city's Medical Officer of Health to write, 'we do not even know accurately the total number of immigrants in Leicester, let alone the size and structure of their families'. Since then some facts about Leicester's population have been revealed through the national census of population in 1981 and a survey, based on a sample of 15.9 per cent of the city's households, made in 1983 and commissioned by the Leicester City Council and the Leicestershire County Council. The 1981 Census points to an immigrant population of about 59,000 while the projection of the data collected by the 1983 *Survey of Leicester* suggests a total of 68,822; that is, 24.1 per cent of the total population of the city. One of the most valuable items in this recent survey is the substantiation of the settlement of Asians largely in two limited areas of the city – Highfields (between the London Road and Humberstone Road) and in Belgrave. Here, in five of the areas selected for analysis by the *Survey*, they account for over 75 per cent of the population.

The 20th century has seen equally striking changes in the countryside

119

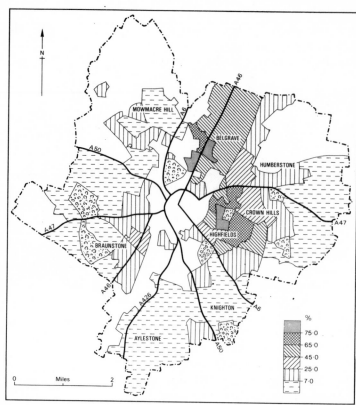

16. People of Asian origin are by far the largest minority ethnic group in Leicester, accounting for 22.1% of the city's population. A sample survey conducted by the City and County Councils in 1983 was based on interviews with 16,700 households, 15.9% of the households in the city. It showed the highest concentration of Asian people in two neighbourhoods — Highfields and Belgrave — where they reached more than 75 per cent.

of Leicestershire and Rutland, of which the most important has been the decline of land under permanent grass. By the time of the First Agricultural Census, taken in 1866, 60 per cent of Leicestershire lay under permanent grass. The trend towards pastoralism, especially the fattening of beef cattle, continued into the 20th century when the *Land Utilisation Survey* of the inter-war years showed that 85 per cent of the county was composed of permanent pasture. The Second World War and the succeeding decades have seen a drastic reversal of this trend — a change in the rural economy that is clearly written on the face of the landscape. By the 1970s only a little more than a third of the countryside of Leicestershire and Rutland remained as permanent grassland. The change towards a system of farming in which cereal crops such as barley are grown in rotation with intensively managed temporary grassland began with the Second World War and the 'plough-up' campaign that had already reduced the pastures of Leicestershire to 41 per cent of the area by 1943. Since World War II the new farming of this century with a lavish use of machinery, a heavy reduction in the labour force and the

120

swallowing up of small farms into bigger units has changed deeply the external appearance of the landscape. Many miles of hedgerows have been ripped out to make larger fields for the huge machines that now work the land, and deep ploughing eradicates the ridge-and-furrow – the hallmark of the Leicestershire countryside at the beginning of the 20th century.

The Second World War began changes of a very different kind in the countryside of Leicestershire and Rutland. The strategy of aerial warfare meant that the East Midland plain was chosen as one of the areas adjacent to the North Sea for the establishment of military aerodromes. Cottesmore and Luffenham, in Rutland, opened as bases for bombers. Four airfields in Leicestershire reflected their position behind the string of offensive bases in Lincolnshire and Rutland. Castle Donington was established as a training unit; Ratcliffe, lying close to the Fosse Way, was used for ferrying aircraft between factories and action stations further east. Rearsby and Bitteswell were also taken over by airfields – the former adjacent to a factory that built light military aircraft and the latter for the testing of Lancaster bombers built in West Midland factories. Only two now survive as active aerodromes. Cottesmore is an important training base for members of the air forces of NATO. Castle Donington has emerged as an airport for Derby, Nottingham and Leicester.

University of Leicester

The communications of the Leicestershire and Rutland countryside have felt the impact of the motorcar, and perhaps even more the heavy lorry, in the post-war years. Railways have all but disappeared from the country to the east of the Soar corridor and the west of Leicestershire has suffered no less. Much of the land where railway tracks ran has been taken into agriculture and at sites within reach of roads, particularly at former stations where empty buildings are available, small industries are sometimes established. The expansion of road transport since the late 1920s caused a steady improvement in the network of communications. The building of Leicester's Charles Street was matched in the countryside by the construction of many miles of dual carriageway, especially on trunk roads such as the A46 to Nottingham, the A50 into the Leicestershire coalfield and parts of the A6. But most of these improvements were patchy, mainly engineered in the years after 1950, and part of schemes that involved the by-passing of villages where the growing volume and speed of traffic had become a nuisance. The one piece of original road building was the opening of Britain's first motorway, between London and Leeds, that cut a fresh course across Charnwood Forest in the north-western section of the county. Leicestershire's only other road designed to move three lines of traffic in each direction is the M69 that forms a link between the M1 and M6.

W.G. Hoskins, in an appreciative guide to Rutland, argues that the delights of that county lie partly in the fact that it escaped the blight of the industrial revolution. Motorways, too, are absent from Rutland's countryside. Only the A1, the busy trunk road that joins London to

121

Edinburgh, skirts Rutland's eastern border. Apart from the military aerodrome, the greatest threat to Rutland's landscape has been the making of a huge reservoir that drowned more than 3,000 acres in the valley of the Gwash above Empingham. The plans aroused great local opposition when this scheme to supply water to Peterborough, Corby, Northampton and Milton Keynes was first proposed, but of late it has been accepted as an important asset for tourism.

The greatest change that lies ahead for Leicestershire, in the last decade of the 20th century, will be the opening up of the recently discovered coalfield whose seams lie buried beneath the Vale of Belvoir at depths between 1,300 and 2,000 feet. Beneath 90 square miles of country to the north of Melton Mowbray lie the energy reserves of the largest coal find made in western Europe since World War II. The first stages of work for this opening up of the field have started at Asfordby; by the end of the century it seems likely that the focus of coal mining will have shifted from west to east in Leicestershire.

The latter half of the 20th century has been the age of the planner in countryside and town. Rutland may have been left unscathed by the industrial revolution, but in the 1970s the doctrine of 'the economy of size' put an official end to this smallest of English counties when it was absorbed into Leicestershire. The result has been a defiant outburst of local feeling of which one expression is the formation of the Rutland Record Society. The proclaimed objective of this society 'is to advise the education of the public in the history of the Ancient County of Rutland'. Is it possible that Rutland might have survived, perhaps enlarged by the acquisition of Stamford and parts of Lincolnshire, if those who devised the extinction of Rutland had been better educated in the history of the county – a history that would have told them about the former extent of Rutland more than a thousand years ago?

The Magazine Gateway, early 15th century, now strangled by the Inner Ring Road

122

Select Bibliography

The following list of titles represents only a minute portion of the sources and publications on the history of Leicestershire and Rutland. They form the background for the writing of the present work. The abbreviations TLAS *and* TLAHS *refer to the Transactions of the Leicestershire Archaeological Society, later the Leicestershire Archaeological and Historical Society.*

Beresford, M. and Hurst, J.G., *Deserted Medieval Villages*, 1971
Billson, C.J., *Medieval Leicester*, 1920
Blake, R.N.E., 'The changing distribution of military airfields in the East Midlands, 1914-80', *The East Midland Geographer*, 7, 1978
Blank, E., *A Guide to Leicestershire Archaeology*, 1970
Bowler, I.R., 'Permanent Grass in Leicestershire: the decline of a traditional land-use and its role in the farming system', *The East Midland Geographer*, 8, 1983
Cameron, K. and Gelling, M., *Place-name evidence for the Anglo-Saxon invasion and Scandinavian settlements*, 1975
Cantor, L.M., 'The Medieval Parks of Leicestershire', *TLAS*, 46, 1970-71
Clemoes, P. and Hughes, K., *England before the Conquest*, 1971
Clinker, C.R., 'The Leicester and Swannington Railway', *TLAS*, 30, 1954
Cornwall, J. (ed.), *Tudor Rutland: The County Community under Henry VIII*, 1980
Courtney, P., 'The Monastic Granges of Leicestershire', *TLAS*, 56, 1980-81
Darby, H.C. and Terrett, I.B., *The Domesday Geography of Midland England*, 1971
Dornier, A. (ed.), *Mercian Studies*, 1977
Elliott, M., *Victorian Leicester*, 1979
Elliott, M., *Leicester: A Pictorial History*, 1983
Ellis, C., *History in Leicester*, 1976
Everard, J.B., *Charnwood Forest*, 1907
Farnham, G.F., *Charnwood Forest and its Historians and the Charnwood Manors*, 1930
Fox, L. and Russell, P., *Leicester Forest*, 1948
Fox-Strangways, C., *The Geology of the Leicestershire and the South Derbyshire Coalfield*, 1907
Greenfield, E. and Webster, G., 'Excavations at High Cross, 1955', *TLAHS*, 40, 1964-65
Hadfield, C., *The Canals of the East Midlands*, 1966
Herbert, A., 'Swithland Slate Headstones', *TLAS*, 1944-45
Hilton, R.H., *The Economic Development of some Leicestershire Estates in the Fourteenth and Fifteenth Centuries*, 1947
Holly, D., 'The Domesday Geography of Leicestershire', *TLAS*, 1938-39
Hoskins, W.G., 'The Fields of Wigston Magna', *TLAS*, 1936-37
Hoskins, W.G., *Midland England*, 1949
Hoskins, W.G., 'The Origin and Rise of Market Harborough', *TLAS*, 1949
Hoskins, W.G., *Essays in Leicestershire History*, 1950
Hoskins, W.G., *Leicestershire (The Making of the English Landscape)*, 1957
Howard-Anderson, P., *Forgotten Railways: The East Midlands*, 1973
Kenyon, K.M., 'Excavations at Breedon-on-the-Hill, Leicestershire', *TLAS*, 26, 1948
Kirby, D.P., 'The Saxon Bishops of Leicester, Lindsey, and Dorchester', *TLAS*, 41, 1965-66
Lamplugh, G.W., *The Geology of the Melton Mowbray District*, 1909

Leleux, R., *The East Midlands* (vol.9 – *A Regional History of the Railways of Great Britain*), 1976

Liddle, P., *Leicestershire Archaeology, the present state of knowledge*, vol. I and II, 1982

McClough, T.H., Dornier, A. and Rutland, R.A., *Anglo-Saxon and Viking Leicestershire*, 1975

McWhirr, A., 'The early military history of the Roman East Midlands', *TLAHS*, 45, 1969-70

McWhirr, A., 'Archaeology in Leicestershire and Rutland', annual reports in *TLAHS*, 1974-79

Morgan, P. (ed.), *Domesday Book, Leicestershire*, 1979

Mounfield, P.R., 'Industrial ablation in the East Midland footwear district', *East Midland Geographer*, 7, 1978

Nichols, J., *History and Antiquities of the County of Leicester*, 1795

Patterson, A.T., *Radical Leicester*, 1954

Pevsner, N., *Leicestershire and Rutland* (The Buildings of England, ed. Elizabeth Williamson), 2nd edition, 1985

Porter, T.R., *The History and Antiquities of Charnwood Forest*, 1842

Pye, N. (ed.), *Leicester and its Region*, 1972

Read, C., *Atlas of Charnwood Borough*, 1978

Royle, S.A., 'The development of Coalville, Leicestershire, in the nineteenth century', *East Midland Geographer*, 7, 1978-81

Sawyer, P.H., 'The density of the Danish Settlement in England', *University of Birmingham Hist. Jnl*, 6, 1958

Simmons, J., 'A Victorian Social Worker: Joseph Dare and the Leicester Domestic Mission', *TLAS*, 46, 1970-71

Simmons, J., *Life in Victorian Leicester*, 1971

Simmons, J., *Leicester, Past and Present*, Vol. 1: *Ancient Borough to 1860*; Vol. 2: *The Modern City*, 1974

Skillington, F.E., 'Post-medieval Cossington', *TLAS*, 19, 1936-37

Survey of Leicester, 1983: Initial Report, 1984

Thomas, C., *Rural Settlement in Roman Britain*, 1966

Thorn, F. (ed.), *Domesday Book, Rutland*, 1980

Todd, M., *The Coritani*, 1973

Traylen, A.R., *Railways in Rutland*, 1980

Turnock, D., 'Railway conversion in Leicestershire, Northamptonshire and adjacent areas', *East Midland Geographer*, 1983

The Victoria History of the Counties of England, Leicestershire, *vols. 1-5, 1907-64*

The Victoria History of the Counties of England, Rutland, vols. 1 and 2, 1908-35

Wacher, J.S., 'Excavations at Breedon-on-the-Hill, Leicestershire', *Antiquaries Jnl*, 44, 1964

Wacher, J.S., 'Excavations at Breedon-on-the-Hill', *TLAHS*, 52, 1976-77

Waites, B., *Exploring Rutland*, 1982

Webster, V.R., 'Cruck-framed buildings of Leicestershire', *TLAS*, 30, 1954

White, W., *History, Gazetteer, and Directory of the Counties of Leicester and Rutland*, 1863

Whitehead, T.H., *The Liassic Ironstones*, 1952

Williams, D., *The Adaptation of Change: essays upon the history of nineteenth-century Leicester and Leicestershire*, 1980

Index

126

education 89, 114; friary 48; Georgian period 87; gilds 51; industry 46-7, 50-1, 92-5; Jewry Wall 25; Jews and 50; local government 51, 87, 110-11, 114-15, 117; medieval period 45-51; navigation 78-9, 88, 95; Newarke Hospital 49-50; Norman period 43-4; population 52, 86-7, 110-14, 119; prehistoric period 16-17, 25; public health 112-13; railway 80-4, 103-9, 112, 116; redevelopment 118; roads 76-7, 118-19, 121; Roman period 21-4, 31, 76; St Clement's parish 45, 47; St George's Church 112; St John's Hospital 46; St Margaret's Church and parish 37, 44, 46, 88, 112; St Martin's Church 44, 45, 51; St Mary de Castro Church 45, 48, 89; St Mary's of the New Work 50; St Michael's Church 45, 47; St Nicholas's Church 25, 31, 44, 45; St Peter's parish 45; Scandinavian elements in 34-5, 37; Wyggeston's Hospital 47
Leicester, earls of 47-50, 66, 76, 97
Leicester Forest 43, 64, 97
Leigh 64
Leighfield Forest 64
Lidington 64
Leland, John 50, 98-9
Life Hill 20
Lincoln, bishop of 44
Littlethorpe 72
Lockington 19, 24, 39
Loddington 30
Long Buckby 80
Long Whatton 39
Loughborough 98-9; industry 93; navigation 78-9, 80, 103; population 86, 89; railway 108-9; roads 76-7
Lount 84-5, 104
Lowesby 63; Hall 68
Lubenham 57
Luffenham 29,121
Lutterworth 90
Lyndon 69

Malore, Ralph 64
Manners family 65
Manton 108
Mapplewell 99
Market Bosworth 18, 52-3, 65, 89
Market Harborough 14, 38; market 57; navigation 79; population 89; roads 77, 90; railway 108
Market Overton 12, 15, 20-1, 25, 28, 80
Markfield 13
Martinsthorpe 69,76
Mary, countess of Derby 50
Massey, Thomas 99
Matilda, Queen 55
Maynard, Viscount 84
Measham 14, 29, 81, 83
Medbourne 22-4, 70
Melbourne 99
Melton Mowbray 35, 90, 122; manor 39-40, 43; market 56; population 42, 86, 89; railway 107-8
Mercia 30-1, 33-6
Moira 14, 91

Moira, earl of 84
Montfort, Simon de 50
Moore, John 73
Mountsorrel 13, 99
Mowsley 52-3

Nailstone 85
Nanpanton 103
Nene, river 30
Nevill family 66
Nevill Holt 66
Newtown Linford 55
Nichols, John 83, 90, 92, 99
Noel family 69
Normanton le Heath 69, 84
North Luffenham 28
Nottingham, earls of 65

Oadby 28, 42, 118
Oakham 15, 40, 43; architecture 90-1; canal 80; castle 48, 55, 66; manor 42; population 41; railway 107; school 89
Oakthorpe 82-3
Offa, king of Mercia 30
Osgathorpe 89
Owston Priory 56

Packington 81
Paget, Thomas 110
Palmer, Thomas 66
Peckleton 76
Pegg and Mason Brothers 95-6
Phillips family 56
Phillips, March 100
Phillips, Sir Ambrose 67
Pick, Perkins 115
Pickwell 68
Pickworth 15, 24, 29
Potter, T. R. 100
Prestgrave Sart 53
Prior, John 83
Pugin, E. W. 65
Pye, Sir Robert 68

Quarles, John 73
Quenby 61, 63
Quorndon 53

Ratby 54
Ratcliffe on the Wreake 16, 17, 121
Rearsby 34, 121
Repton 33
Richard III 67
Richards, William 96
Ridlington 42, 55, 64
Robert, count of Meulon 50
Robin-a-Tiptoe 20
Rotherby 34
Rothley 39, 40, 109
Rowley Fields 28
Rutland, dukes and earls of 65, 69
Rutland Forest 64
Rutland Water 69, 122

Saddington 30, 79
Sapcote 24

128